INSIGHTS

**The MIT Press Essential Knowledge Series**

# BEHAVIORAL
# INSIGHTS

MICHAEL HALLSWORTH AND
ELSPETH KIRKMAN

The MIT Press | Cambridge, Massachusetts | London, England

This book was set in Chaparral Pro by New Best-set Typesetters Ltd. Printed
and bound in the United States of America.

Library of Congress Cataloging-in-Publication Data

Names: Hallsworth, Michael, author. | Kirkman, Elspeth, author.
Title: Behavioral insights / Michael Hallsworth and Elspeth Kirkman.
Description: Cambridge, Massachusetts : The MIT Press, [2020] | Series:
   The MIT press essential knowledge series | Includes bibliographical
   references and index.
Identifiers: LCCN 2020000394 | ISBN 9780262539401 (paperback)
Subjects: LCSH: Political planning—Psychological aspects. | Social
   planning—Psychological aspects. | Policy sciences—Psychological
   aspects. | Psychology, Industrial.
Classification: LCC HN28 .H28 2020 | DDC 361.1—dc23
LC record available at https://lccn.loc.gov/2020000394

10   9   8   7   6   5   4   3   2   1

# CONTENTS

# SERIES FOREWORD

The MIT Press Essential Knowledge series offers accessible, concise, beautifully produced pocket-size books on topics of current interest. Written by leading thinkers, the books in this series deliver expert overviews of subjects that range from the cultural and the historical to the scientific and the technical.

In today's era of instant information gratification, we have ready access to opinions, rationalizations, and superficial descriptions. Much harder to come by is the foundational knowledge that informs a principled understanding of the world. Essential Knowledge books fill that need. Synthesizing specialized subject matter for nonspecialists and engaging critical topics through fundamentals, each of these compact volumes offers readers a point of access to complex ideas.

Many of us have suddenly stopped and asked ourselves, "Why did I just do that?" We may have paused, looked around, and realized that we made it halfway home while our thoughts were elsewhere. Or maybe we sat next to a purchase that we now wonder if we really want or need, having been guided toward it effortlessly by prompts and reassurances.

These instances highlight that our behavior is often influenced by factors that lie outside our conscious awareness. This is not necessarily a problem; we would find it very hard to function if we had to consciously register and approve every single thing we do. But often we tend to underestimate the importance of this "automatic" side of our behavior—and so do governments or other organizations. The result may be ineffective policies, products, or plans.

The behavioral insights approach tries to address this problem by taking the latest evidence on what influences behavior, and then applying these insights to practical issues. Since the approach also prioritizes evaluating the impact of its interventions, we can know exactly how it has made a difference to tangible problems. As a result, the use of behavioral insights by governments, businesses, and individuals has exploded over the last ten years.

But there have also been many questions about whether the behavioral insights approach is a reliable one, whether it can tackle the big issues facing society, and whether it poses serious ethical questions. There is also much confusion about what the term "behavioral insights" actually means. This book addresses these questions by presenting the history, current practice, and future directions of behavioral insights.

Chapter 1 outlines the core features of the approach: a concern with practical issues; the use of evidence about human behavior to develop solutions for these issues; and the use of experimentation to evaluate the impact of these solutions. We show that this approach is best understood as a lens that allows us to see policies, programs, and services in a new light. Chapter 2 charts the history of the behavioral insights approach, which was born when three strands of thought came together: behavioral economics, dual-process theories in psychology, and a shift in how governments think about behavior. We explain how and why the period since 2010 has seen explosive growth in the use of the approach. Chapter 3 gives five brief examples of behavioral insights in practice.

Chapter 4 gives an overview of how to apply behavioral insights by working through a real example of increasing attendance at recruitment fairs by those looking for work. We include ten steps that cover identifying the scope and relevant behaviors, implementing and evaluating the intervention, and considering next steps. Chapter 5 is devoted to questions and criticisms. We consider the limitations of what the approach delivers on a practical level, including the longevity of its effects and its impact on high-level policy. We look at limitations of the relevant theories, and weaknesses in the evidence base. Finally, we consider whether the behavioral insights approach is ethical or acceptable. Chapter 6 looks to the future. We argue that in order to endure, the behavioral insights approach needs to consolidate and strengthen its evidence base and to prioritize new techniques and applications. Finally, it needs to integrate itself into standard practices for organizations—ironically, true success may come when we stop talking about "behavioral insights" as a distinct idea.

# ACKNOWLEDGMENTS

We thank Owain Service, David Halpern, Luke Hydrick, and Adam Oliver for their comments on the manuscript for this book. We thank all our colleagues at the Behavioural Insights Team over the years. We thank Bob Prior for being a great editor, and the staff at the MIT Press for their production of the book.

Elspeth thanks Melanie Skipp-Kirkman for her patience and support while this book was being written (especially while she was heavily pregnant with our amazing daughter, Imogen, at the end!). She also takes this official opportunity to thank Sue, Alan, and Annie Kirkman for their lifelong support and love.

Michael thanks Ellen Hallsworth for all her guidance and encouragement, which were essential to the completion of the book, and Alice Hallsworth for being a welcome distraction from writing it. He also thanks Alan and Marion Hallsworth and Ceri Rahman for everything they've done for him over the years.

# INTRODUCING BEHAVIORAL INSIGHTS

The behavioral insights approach applies evidence about human behavior to practical problems. Behavioral insights can give a realistic account of how and why we act the way we do, allowing us to design or redesign policies, products, and services accordingly. The results of this approach have led to its adoption by governments, institutions, and businesses across the globe. This book explains the main principles of a behavioral insights approach, why it has proved so popular, and what it can achieve.

Let's start by discussing what is new about the approach: it offers a challenge to received wisdom about how decisions are made. Individuals, governments, and businesses often assume that our behavior is governed mostly by deliberate, considered reactions to the information and incentives we encounter. In this view, people take note of all relevant knowledge, carefully weigh up the costs and benefits of each available option, and make the choice that they think maximizes benefits to themselves (or those they care about).

In contrast, the key "insight" of behavioral insights is that much of our behavior is nonconscious, habitual, and driven by cues in our environment or the way in which choices are presented. We are capable of making decisions in a considered, deliberate way, but this happens less often than we assume. Instead, our actions are guided by mental shortcuts or simple "rules of thumb"—for example, "do what everyone else is doing" or "take the middle option." These shortcuts are often triggered automatically—outside our conscious awareness—by features of the choices or situations that we encounter.

As a result, aspects of the context or the way a decision is presented may shape our behavior much more than we realize. Consider our eating behavior, which we use as an extended example throughout this first chapter. Since people use the presence of a salad as a shortcut for "healthy" when judging food options, adding a salad to a hamburger meal actually makes us think it has 12.6 percent fewer calories than the same meal with no salad.[1] The amount we eat is influenced in similar ways. Doubling a serving size means people eat one-third more, on average,[2] and the cues surrounding our food also matter: bigger food packages and larger serving utensils mean more food is eaten.[3]

Much of our behavior is nonconscious, habitual, and driven by cues in our environment or the way in which choices are presented.

While these automatic reactions take place outside our conscious awareness, often they have developed as efficient and powerful ways to accomplish our goals. Consider how much more difficult our lives would be if we had to focus deliberately on each element of tying our shoelaces every morning, or to carefully weigh up the pros and cons of absolutely every food purchase we ever made. This kind of "fast" thinking is what allows us to make thousands of successful judgments and decisions every day, without even realizing that we are doing so.

Nevertheless, our lack of awareness also has costs: it means that we usually do not recognize the way these processes are shaping our behavior. In one study, more than half of people who had been deliberately served between 500 g and 1,000 g of macaroni and cheese for lunch (over the course of a month) failed to notice that their portions had varied at all.[4] Even if we do notice such things, we often come up with alternative explanations for our behavior. For example, we may claim that we ate more than usual because we happened to be particularly hungry. But the same studies show that's not true: portion sizes, not hunger, cause the increased eating.

Whether we are examining food intake or any other kind of decision, the headline is this: if we do not understand our behavior accurately, then we are unlikely to adopt the best personal plans or public policies to achieve our goals. We will develop systems and strategies that depend on us pausing and deliberating when the evidence shows we will not. Behavioral insights can show us what is really driving our actions in these cases. In doing so, the approach provides explanations and predictions that guide us to more effective courses of action.

Having discussed the "insights" part of our topic, we now want to explain the importance of focusing on "behavior." We are interested in what people actually do; changes in stated attitudes, beliefs, and intentions are important, but they may not go along with changes in behavior.[5] And we emphasize direct observation because of the problems with people reporting their own behavior. People often do not correctly remember what they have done and inaccurately predict what they are going to do. This may be partly driven by the desire to maintain a positive self-image. Even if they have such knowledge, they may tailor their reports to reflect what they think is socially desirable or what a researcher wants to hear.[6]

For example, one national study asked adults to recall how much physical activity they had done over the previous month. A smaller group of those who responded also wore an accelerometer for the week following the survey. An accelerometer directly measures how much people move. When self-reporting, 39 percent of men and 29 percent of women said that they achieved the minimum recommended level of physical activity. But the data from the accelerometers showed that only 6 percent of men and 4 percent of women had done this in reality.[7]

In a nutshell, the behavioral insights approach brings together evidence of how conscious deliberation interacts with nonconscious processes to shape behavior. But it also builds on this evidence to propose new solutions, as we show in the following.

## What Does the Behavioral Insights Approach Offer?

To show how behavioral insights can suggest new ways of doing things, let's stay with the topic of eating. Suppose policymakers decided that overeating was a problem that required action. In this situation, behavioral insights can enhance the main policy options available to governments and citizens: information (telling people about how to perform or avoid a behavior and why they should do so), incentives (changing the costs or benefits resulting from a behavior), and legislation (preventing or requiring certain behaviors by law). We give a brief tour of each of these areas.

### Information

In general terms, the traditional approach to providing information about eating has been to tell people about what foods they should or should not be consuming. However, since many of our food choices are driven by habits and take place outside our conscious awareness, an improved understanding of the risks and benefits of certain foods may only have limited impact on behavior. In fact, providing information can backfire. For example, one study found that people were actually more likely to take a drug when several possible side effects were presented to them, as opposed to a single one, because of the way we perceive risks.[8]

With these principles in mind, a behavioral insights approach might instead help people adopt new pragmatic "rules of thumb" that focus on creating new habits. For example, we can create simple plans to make it less likely that we are exposed to tempting food—like "if a waiter asks if I'd like to see the dessert menu, then I will ask for a coffee."[9] This kind of planning, which can end up creating new habits, has been shown to be effective across many studies.[10] In other words, a behavioral insights approach would suggest that information should focus less on what people should eat and more on how they actually eat. Dietary guidance does not need to be abandoned; instead, there should be a shift toward how that guidance can be turned into action.

### Incentives

Let's turn to the next tool in the policy toolbox: incentives. In relation to food consumption, a lot of attention has focused on how taxes can be used to increase the price of unhealthy foods. The idea is to shift people's purchases away from unhealthy foods—and potentially toward healthy ones—just as tax increases led to lower tobacco use. For example, Mexico, Chile, and various cities in the United States have introduced taxes on sugared drinks with this goal in mind.

Trying to influence consumers' purchases in this way is worth considering. But a behavioral insights approach suggests that taxation could be used in a different, and potentially more powerful, way: to incentivize reformulation. Studies show that serving meals with one-quarter fewer calories led people to reduce their energy intake by the same amount.[11] In other words, people did not compensate by eating more food, nor did they feel less full than people who had consumed the full-calorie version. Therefore, reformulating foods to remove calories is a powerful way of addressing overeating. Consumers will not have to make an effort to change their behavior: they can buy the same products, but face fewer negative health effects.

This goal to drive producers to reformulate products was at the heart of the UK's sugared drink tax (Soft Drinks Industry Levy), announced in 2016. This policy had two features that showed that the main target was the behavior of producers, rather than consumers. First, the tax escalated according to sugar levels in the drink. Any drinks with less than 5 g of sugar per 100 ml were exempt from the tax; any drinks with more than 8 g of sugar per 100 ml were taxed at the highest rate; any drinks in the middle were taxed at a lower rate. The tiers were an important innovation. Previous attempts to introduce taxes on sugared drinks did not have tiers; they were just applied by volume: the larger the drink, the more tax that was applied. In contrast, creating tiers to the tax gave producers an incentive to reformulate their products, while the cost of doing so was reduced because the levels were set so that most existing products were not too far away from one of the thresholds. Second, the tax would not come into force for two years, giving producers the time needed to reformulate their products.

The tax influenced the behavior of producers as expected. They quickly reformulated the content of both famous-name and own-brand drinks. In just three years, the amount of sugar sold per person from sodas fell by 30 percent, equating to nearly 5 g per person per day. This happened because the market changed: the total volume sales of drinks that were subject to the tax fell by 50 percent, while the sale of exempt low and zero-sugar drinks rose by 40 percent. The great majority of this change was due to reformulation, rather than consumers switching their choices.[12] Thinking differently about behavior led to a policy where consumer inertia contributed to success, not failure, and where taxation was structured so that businesses were influenced to do the heavy lifting instead.

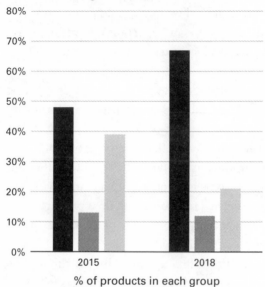

## Sugar Content of Products

Figure 1

### Legislation

Finally, we can see how behavioral insights can change the way we think about the laws governments make and how they enforce them. In terms of eating, a common proposal is to legally require food manufacturers and sellers to display nutrient information on packages and menus. Many of these laws specify the exact way that the information should be shown. A common option (adopted by the United States and the European Union) is to rely mostly or completely on displaying numbers, like calories. The idea is that people will keep track of their calorie consumption and make choices on that basis. But is this a realistic or optimal approach?

Again, the evidence from behavioral science suggests not. Let's put aside the problem that only a minority of people (39 percent of women and 24 percent of men in the UK, for example) know how many calories they should be consuming daily in the first place.[13] The main issue is that people filter and process food information using rapid mental shortcuts. Numerical calorie information does not align with these shortcuts; instead, it relies on us deliberately weighing up the calories and adding them to an ongoing tally. Labeling that taps into fast, intuitive decision making appears to work better. For example, traffic-light labeling uses a simple color system that can be interpreted at a glance, without conscious engagement. Several studies have shown that traffic lights have a bigger impact on food choices than simple calorie counts, which often do not appear to have any effect.[14] The German government has announced that it will introduce a single traffic-light system for nutrition labeling ("Nutriscore") that uses these principles.

The main point underlying these examples is: make sure that policies or programs are informed by the best evidence about what influences behavior. If you are going to introduce a law, understand the option that is most likely to change behavior. If you are introducing incentives, set their timing, size, structure, and conditions to maximize their effect. When creating an information campaign, take into account how we notice and process information. In general, ensure that you have a realistic understanding of what does and will influence behavior, and why.

### Behavioral Insights as a Lens

The behavioral insights approach is perhaps best understood as a lens through which we see policies, programs, and services—and that enables us to introduce new options, enhance existing ones, and reassess current activity.

The new options offered by behavioral insights have tended to attract the most attention. As the case of food consumption shows, the evidence may have surprising implications that cut against our assumptions and open up new ideas. As discussed later, many of these ideas may deal with the way that choices are structured—what has been called "choice architecture."[15] For example, many people display a "compromise effect," whereby they use a mental shortcut of "go for the middle option."[16] Awareness of this compromise effect may reveal new approaches. Studies have shown that soft-drink consumption can be reduced by removing the largest cup size on offer and adding a smaller one at the bottom of the scale, since people often choose the middle option, regardless of its size.[17] And thinking more carefully about the order in which options are presented offers another new opportunity. For example, sales of a sugared soft drink declined when it was moved from first to third in the list of options in electronic touchscreen kiosks in 622 McDonald's restaurants.[18]

However, the behavioral insights approach does not just offer new tools. Using it as a lens can also, for example, reveal how existing actions may be creating unintended and undesirable behaviors; it could highlight the biases that affect policymakers themselves; it could show the flawed assumptions about behavior in a proposed rule and show how it can be changed; or it could show that the best solution may not be attempting to change behavior at all, but rather redesigning services around what is already occurring.

This point is worth stressing because it counters some misperceptions about the true scope and value of behavioral insights. One is that the behavioral insights approach is just an alternative to more traditional instruments like information, taxation, or legislation—and has nothing to say about these options. As just shown, behavioral insights can provide recommendations about how these approaches should be put into practice that can make the difference between success and failure. Another misperception is that the approach just deals with tweaks or incremental changes—or that it is focused solely on individuals' decisions. As shown earlier, this approach can be used to completely rethink and redesign systems or policies like sugared drink taxation. A final misperception is to see the behavioral insights approach just as an optional extra "tool" that policymakers can use (or not) if they feel like it. But since most government policies are concerned with influencing behavior (from murder laws to sex education), behavioral insights will have something to say about most policies.

Figure 2 brings these concepts together by showing the wide possible "field" in which behavioral insights can be applied. Along the bottom axis we give the simplified set of activities we mentioned earlier: information, incentives, and regulation. Along the side axis we have two basic ways that behavioral insights can be used: tactically, to make changes to the way in which a policy is implemented, and strategically, to structure the fundamental aspects of the policy itself. We populate the resulting space with some examples to show the different possible applications.

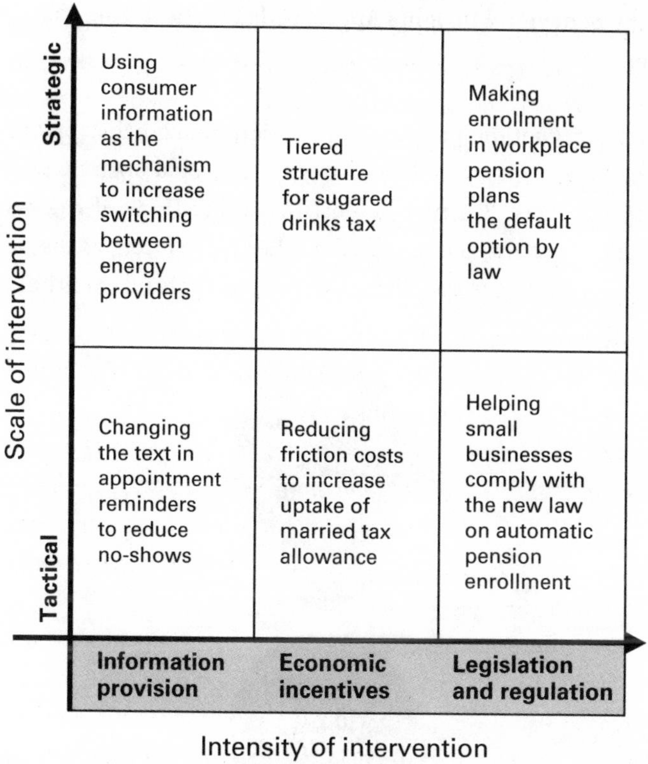

|  | Information provision | Economic incentives | Legislation and regulation |
|---|---|---|---|
| **Strategic** | Using consumer information as the mechanism to increase switching between energy providers | Tiered structure for sugared drinks tax | Making enrollment in workplace pension plans the default option by law |
| **Tactical** | Changing the text in appointment reminders to reduce no-shows | Reducing friction costs to increase uptake of married tax allowance | Helping small businesses comply with the new law on automatic pension enrollment |

Scale of intervention (vertical axis)

Intensity of intervention (horizontal axis)

Figure 2

## The Behavioral Insights Approach Is Practical and Empirical

We have outlined the evidence underpinning behavioral insights and discussed how that evidence could open up new perspectives. But that potential is realized only if the evidence is complemented by the other two aspects of the behavioral insights approach: it is also practical and empirical.

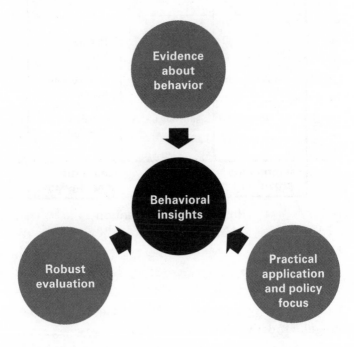

Figure 3

By practical, we mean there is a focus on finding specific solutions to problems that individuals, organizations, or governments consider to be important. In chapter 4 we detail a process for applying behavioral insights. This process begins by identifying the relevant behaviors that need to start, stop, continue, or change, before developing an understanding of the barriers and enablers to these behaviors. Once the nature of the issue has been diagnosed, there is a process of designing concrete proposals to influence the relevant behaviors.

Although this activity will be guided by a nuanced understanding of the academic literature, and will attempt to apply existing findings faithfully, its main concern is pragmatic. How can we develop a realistic plan that will be sensitive to the demands of people tasked with delivering services, or that will not make infeasible demands on the individuals using them? How can we build something that is resilient to the pressures it will experience?

Similarly, the behavioral insights approach focuses on the details of exactly how any new proposal will be realized in practice. Since individuals are highly responsive to how choices are presented, whether a behavior occurs may depend on the particular choice of words in a message, or the precise number of steps required to complete an action. Some of the most well-known examples of behavioral insights are of this kind, and their popularity has led some observers to claim that a behavioral insights approach just ends up tweaking existing practices. But, as already noted, the contribution of behavioral insights extends much further.

The final feature of the behavioral insights approach is that it is empirical. There is a strong emphasis on gathering evidence to determine the effect of any intervention informed by behavioral science. Some of this drive to evaluate follows on directly from the arguments just made about how people are affected by features of presentation and context—that is, how things are realized in practice. Although we can use behavioral science to make general predictions about how people will react, human behavior is complex: Many factors may influence a particular decision. Even if we are relying on apparently strong evidence, features of an intervention (presentation, timing) will need to be adapted to fit the new context. We cannot be sure that some combination of word or images won't backfire in ways we had not anticipated. And the fact that unexpected results have emerged often breeds a streak of skepticism and humility about how much we still do not know about human behavior.

Such skepticism and humility mean that the behavioral insights approach prioritizes randomized controlled trials (RCTs) that measure behavioral outcomes in real-world settings. We have already discussed why there is a focus on influencing behavior, rather than attitudes or beliefs. We explain RCTs in more detail later, but their core principle is that using random chance (like the throw of a die) to divide people into groups means that these groups have similar characteristics on average—similar age, wealth, location, attitudes, and so on. This similarity means that we would expect the two groups to behave alike if just left alone. Therefore, if we introduce an intervention to just one of the groups, we can say that any changes in that group's behavior are due to the intervention—rather than to any other cause. Running an RCT is the standard method for working out whether medicines are effective: one group is given the trial medicine, while the other is given a sugar pill (a placebo).

In addition, it's worth explaining why the focus on real-world settings is important. Many randomized controlled trials that measure behavior take place in laboratories. Laboratories are very useful because they create conditions that allow interventions to be executed cleanly and permit results to be measured precisely. But these conditions may also mean that people act differently from how they do in the real world.[19] For example, experiments that try to understand tax compliance often create artificial game-like situations, played for much lower stakes, under close observation, using student populations with no experience of paying taxes.[20] Since the focus of behavioral insights is on real-world problems, there has been a strong desire to check whether results created in laboratories hold true in these settings. As a result, the behavioral insights approach does not just consume and apply research; it also attempts to create new knowledge of "what works" in practice.

There is a caveat, however: it may not always be possible to run an evaluation that features randomization, real-world settings, and direct measures of behavior. If we are introducing a policy that deals with national-level systems (e.g., the UK's sugared drinks tax), then randomization is not possible. If we are dealing with behaviors that are very difficult to observe (e.g., intimate partner violence), then direct measures of behavior may be challenging. Sometimes there may be ethical barriers to running experiments in real-world settings, and simulated ones are the next best option. In other words, not every behavioral insights project is evaluated using an RCT—and not everything that is evaluated using an RCT falls under the umbrella of behavioral insights. But there should always be a drive to ask: "How sure are we that this will work? How can we test what impact we may be having?"

## The Impact of Behavioral Insights

We have introduced the core features of behavioral insights: a concern with practical problems; the application of evidence about human behavior to create new potential solutions to these problems; and the use of experimentation to evaluate the impact of these solutions on behavior. Our one-sentence definition is: *The behavioral insights approach uses evidence of the conscious and nonconscious drivers of human behavior to address practical issues.*

This approach has proved to be attractive and powerful. In just eight years, ten million more employees have started saving for a UK workplace pension, and private-sector coverage has gone from 42 percent to 85 percent, simply because the default option was changed to automatic enrollment.[21] Around the world, health systems are finding that giving social norm feedback to doctors can help reduce unnecessary antibiotic prescribing, helping to preserve this vital resource for future generations.[22] And a series of studies has shown that simple, low-cost text messages sent to parents and students can improve student attendance and achievement.[23]

Much more can be done, of course, as we explain later. But this impact has attracted considerable attention. Since the term "behavioral insights" was coined by the UK government's Behavioural Insights Team in 2010, the approach has (in the words of the Organisation for Economic Co-operation and Development, or OECD) "taken root in many ways across many countries around the world and across a wide range of sectors and policy areas."[24] Dedicated teams have been created in the governments of countries such as the United States, India, France, Japan, Qatar, Chile, Canada, the Netherlands, Singapore,

The behavioral insights approach uses evidence of the conscious and nonconscious drivers of human behavior to address practical issues.

Australia, Germany, and many more. The World Bank, the European Commission, the United Nations, and the OECD have joined them. Some of the world's largest companies—like Google, Walmart, and Swiss Re—have created their own in-house units to provide behavioral insights. Other organizations, networks, centers, events, books, and academic journals have grown up to apply, develop, and debate the approach. Some of the ideas have also been adopted by individuals to better achieve their own goals. In the next chapter we explore how all this happened.

# THE HISTORY AND THOUGHT BEHIND BEHAVIORAL INSIGHTS

Many of the concepts we are discussing have a long lineage, even if they appear to be new. Twenty-four centuries ago, Plato's dialogues gave several examples of how our perceptions are dependent on context, which we would now express in the language of "framing." Francis Bacon's 1620 work *Novum Organum* gives a great account of "confirmation bias" in the lines "once a human intellect has adopted an opinion . . . it draws everything else in to confirm and support it." In *Mansfield Park*, Jane Austen documents the "mere exposure effect" in the observation that the Bertram sisters come to find the initially "plain" Henry Crawford more attractive at each visit.[1]

We want to acknowledge this history because we can only offer a very brief account of it. We pull out three strands of Western thought that are essential for understanding behavioral insights. First, we explain the evolution of "behavioral economics." Then, we outline the most relevant contributions from psychology. The final strand considers changes in the way governments think about the behaviors of those they govern. We then bring these strands together to show how the field of behavioral insights itself has developed and spread in the last fifteen years. While many of the ideas have old origins, the way they are now being combined and applied is something new.

## The Evolution of Behavioral Economics

The Enlightenment of the eighteenth century foregrounded human reason as a powerful force for knowledge and progress. As part of this general change, some thinkers began to examine how individuals can use their powers of reason to achieve their goals. In this vein, the philosopher Jeremy Bentham developed the core idea of trying to maximize "utility," which he broadly saw as someone's benefit, well-being, or pleasure. By 1836, John Stuart Mill had expressed an "arbitrary definition of man, as a being who inevitably does that by which he may obtain the greatest amount of necessaries, conveniences, and luxuries, with the smallest quantity of labour and physical self-denial with which they can be obtained."[2] Of course, achieving one's own goals may be in conflict with those of other people, or society as a whole.[3] Contemporaries of Mill who were critical of this definition labeled the person it depicts as "*homo economicus*," or "economic man."[4]

As the field of economics developed in the late nineteenth and early twentieth centuries, scholars began to flesh out the idea of *homo economicus* into a coherent theory of behavior. The main principles of this "rational choice theory" are that we have coherent and stable preferences, we consider the full range of information relevant to a decision, and we use that information to calculate the option that best fulfills our preferences.[5] Economists always recognized that this approach did not capture the full range of human action, but rather that it was a simplified account that produced useful predictions and analyses. However, as their focus shifted to building sophisticated mathematical models based on the theory's core elements, less attention was paid to broader factors influencing behavior (such as the role of sympathy, which had been emphasized by earlier economists like Adam Smith).

Herbert Simon did not follow this path. Simon was a polymath who made groundbreaking contributions to organizational behavior, computer science, psychology, and economics. The way humans make decisions is a common thread throughout his work. In contrast to rational choice theory, Simon proposed *bounded rationality.*[6] Bounded rationality states that instead of a comprehensive search for the option that offers maximum benefits, people "satisfice": They use mental shortcuts and rules of thumb (or "heuristics") to find and select an option that is satisfactory, rather than optimal.

For example, consider someone who has to choose between two restaurants to dine in. From the perspective of rational choice theory, the optimal strategy would be to gather and analyze all available information on the price of food, its quality, the ambience, and other relevant factors at each establishment. In contrast, someone who is satisficing might use the heuristic that "the busier restaurant is probably better," combined with a quick look to check that the prices are acceptable, on the basis that that will probably produce a good enough decision. People satisfice because they have limited cognitive resources and have to make decisions quickly in complex environments.

The restaurant choice example illustrates Simon's view that satisficing is generally a useful strategy and fares well compared to optimizing. Clearly, this view cuts against the main tenets of rational choice theory. However, despite winning a Nobel Prize in Economics, Simon had little impact on the economics profession.[7] Bounded rationality was seen as something that was true, perhaps inconvenient, but ultimately not sufficiently important to offer a fundamental challenge.

That challenge was to come a little later. In the early 1970s, the psychologists Daniel Kahneman and Amos Tversky began to run experiments that tested how far people's decisions actually matched the predictions of rational choice theory. These experiments were entertaining, memorable, and easy to understand (see the brief account of "lingering colonoscopies" in the next chapter). They also showed that people's actual judgments and decisions deviated from those of *homo economicus* because heuristics and "biases" influenced their choices.[8] Perhaps most importantly, they claimed that these deviations were systematic and therefore could be predicted and incorporated into economists' models.

We do not cover the specific examples and insights from Kahneman and Tversky's work in depth, since there are many good accounts out there already—not least by Daniel Kahneman himself in his best-selling book *Thinking, Fast and Slow*.[9] One of the simpler experiments concerns how we bring information to mind. Kahneman and Tversky selected five consonants (K, L, N, R, V), all of which appear more often as the third letter of a word than as the first letter of a word. They then showed each of these consonants to people and asked them: Is this letter more likely to appear as the first or third letter in a word?

Participants generally thought that these letters were more likely to be in the first position than in the third. On average, they thought the letters came up twice as much in the first position (e.g., "lion") than in the third (e.g., "milk").[10] This is despite the fact that, in reality, they were all more likely to be the third letter. The explanation for this result is simple: it is easier to think of words that begin with a particular letter than ones that have a particular letter buried in them. This observation then gets filtered through a mental shortcut: the easier it is to think of something, the more common that something must be.

Kahneman and Tversky called this the "availability heuristic," on the basis that certain ideas are more "available" to our mind than others. This is what is happening when people are concerned about air travel because they can easily bring to mind images of horrific crashes, when the objective risks from flying are much lower than other options. Of course, *homo economicus* should not let such things influence her choices. She should be assessing all the relevant information, regardless of how easily it comes to mind.

Kahneman and Tversky present many other examples of how rational choice theory does not capture real decisions. When assessing risks, decision makers are meant to weigh the chance of gains against the chance of losses to see whether the net result is likely to be positive (known as "expected utility theory"). In fact, potential losses weigh much more heavily in such a decision than potential gains—Tversky and Kahneman claim that in order for someone to agree to a gamble, the amount they could win needs to be about twice as much as the amount they could lose.

In the right circumstances, we are even influenced by whether the description of a choice emphasizes gains or losses. For example, Tversky coauthored a study showing that 84 percent of doctors chose surgery over radiation if they were told that "The one-month survival rate [for this surgery] is 90 percent," but only 50 percent did so if they were told that "There is a 10 percent mortality in the first month." The two statements communicate the same information, but one frames the choice in terms of gains, and the other in terms of losses.[11]

Although this research has similarities to Herbert Simon's work (e.g., the importance of mental shortcuts), it was presented rather differently. Kahneman and Tversky framed the results in terms of errors or divergence from *homo economicus*, published their work in economics journals, and provided quantitative estimates of the impact of their findings. Even so, it is not clear how much their work would have truly influenced economics without some effective advocates from within the discipline itself. Fortunately, they had these.

Richard Thaler had encountered their findings in 1976, and immediately saw their relevance to a set of his own observations that were puzzling from the standpoint of rational choice theory. Thaler embarked on several collaborations with the two psychologists, as well as developing his own concepts, which began to offer alternative explanations for economic behavior. His high-profile series of articles on "anomalies" began to recruit a critical mass of researchers, who started to come together, attract the support of influential institutions, and create a new generation of researchers—who, in turn, developed more sophisticated accounts of what began to be called "behavioral economics."

This label reflects the empirical focus on how people actually behave, rather than on how rational choice theories predict they should. One quick final example captures the essence of the field: Thaler's concept of "mental accounting," which concerns how people categorize and keep track of money. One of the principles of *homo economicus* is that she treats money as "fungible": it can easily be moved to pay for any goods or services; funds are not attached to any particular purpose. Money is money. In reality, people do assign pots of money to certain uses (e.g., "the rent money") and do not like to move money between those pots.

A good example concerns the way people pay for car fuel in the United States. In the United States, gasoline is sold in three varieties of increasing price and quality. In 2008, the price of gasoline fell by around 50 percent. This meant that people had more disposable income and, in line with rational choice theory, could spend that money however they wanted to—chocolate bars, cigarettes, pet food, whatever. But economists who studied real transaction data found that people were actually shifting toward getting the more expensive kind of gasoline instead.[12] Since they had a mental budget of, say, $50 for gasoline, and

Behavioral economics has an empirical focus on how people actually behave, rather than on how rational choice theories predict they should.

had room within that budget, they filled it up. Importantly, purchases of other items like milk and orange juice at the same stores were not affected: people did not buy more expensive brands of these products with their additional income, only gasoline. Of course, it could be that premium gasoline is exactly what people really want to spend their extra money on. But in general, having more income produces only a very small shift toward buying premium.

We are not saying that mental accounts are unwise or unhelpful as such—they can be, but equally they can be the opposite. Governments may want to help people to create mental accounts that help them fulfill their goals (like saving for college) or provide safety nets in the case of turmoil. Instead, the main point is that the importance of mental accounting needs to be recognized—if it is ignored or dismissed as irrelevant, then policies and plans are likely to go astray.

Behavioral economics has been particularly concerned with these kinds of individual-level decisions—but not exclusively so. For example, it has offered new things to say about how and why John Maynard Keynes's "animal spirits" (1936) cause markets to show unexpected and erratic behaviors, like bubbles, panics, and crashes.[13] And the field developed in other ways as well. One trend was a move to greater experimentation in real-world settings, partly to see whether biases would disappear if people had "skin in the game"—the answer was "no."[14] Another

was the trend toward applying these ideas to policy problems, whether they were increasing organ donation rates[15]
or helping people save for their retirement.[16] But at this
point we need to pause, and return to this trend once we
have explored a different history that bends toward a similar point.


## The Path toward Dual-Process Theories

So far, we have explored how the Enlightenment foregrounded the power of conscious human reasoning. Other
thinkers, however, were interested in the aspects of human conduct that seemed to evade consciousness. Already
in 1890, one of the "founding fathers" of psychology, William James, was emphasizing just how much power habitual and automatic processes exert over our behavior and
concluding that this ability to do complex things without
thinking was fundamentally helpful:

> The more of the details of our daily life we can hand
> over to the effortless custody of automatism, the
> more our higher powers of mind will be set free for
> their own proper work. There is no more miserable
> human being than one in whom nothing is habitual
> but indecision, and for whom the lighting of every
> cigar, the drinking of every cup, the time of rising

going to bed every day, and the beginning of ₍a₎ bit of work, are subjects of express volitional deliberation. Full half the time of such a man goes to the deciding, or regretting, of matters which ought to be so ingrained in him as practically not to exist for his consciousness at all.[17]

Around the same time, Wilhelm Wundt (who built the first psychology lab in 1879) was proposing a distinction between voluntary and involuntary action, with the first being "slow, effortful and conscious," while the second "requires little effort and operates beyond conscious control."[18] You will recognize that what James and Wundt were proposing is quite similar to the behavioral insights principles in chapter 1. However, it would be another hundred years before psychologists started to agree on the relative roles of automatic and reflective drivers of behavior, and how they interact. This hundred-year jump skips over many events (including the rise and fall of "behaviorism" in the mid-twentieth century) and lands us at about the time that Kahneman and Tversky started to run their experiments in the 1970s.

At this point, many theories of behavior were based on the principle that people's attitudes, motivations, and intentions strongly determined their actions. The fact that one of the most popular was called the "theory of reasoned action" perhaps backs up our point. However, from this point on, psychologists and neuroscientists began to produce increasing amounts of empirical evidence for the importance of nonconscious drivers of behavior.[19] Kahneman and Tversky's experiments on mental shortcuts were part of this trend, but far from the whole story. Another high-profile example was the work of the social psychologist Robert Cialdini. His popular book *Influence* (1984) showed how examples of everyday persuasion (say, by salespeople or businesses) could be explained by people's unthinking response to certain kinds of situations or requests. This accumulating evidence led many psychologists to converge on dual-process theories to explain behavior.[20]

The essence of the dual-process perspective is that humans have two main ways of thinking that influence our behavior.[21] One is controlled, slow, deliberative, reflective, and self-aware. It requires focused effort from us—and therefore we may have limited capacity or inclination to make decisions this way. This is the process that is taking place when we are planning an unfamiliar journey or learning a foreign language. In the preceding quote, William James called it "express volitional deliberation"; we call it the Reflective System.

The other process is uncontrolled, fast, intuitive, and unconscious. Since it occurs outside our awareness, it also requires little to no effort from us, and therefore we can make many decisions this way without fatigue. This is the

Humans have two main ways of thinking that influence our behavior. One is controlled, slow, deliberative, reflective, and self-aware. The other is uncontrolled, fast, intuitive, and unconscious.

process at play when we are taking our daily commute, speaking our native language, or performing a habitual action. In fact, it includes instinctive reactions that we may not closely with associate with the term "thinking" as such, like judging the speed of an oncoming vehicle or flinching when a plane hits turbulence. William Wundt called it "involuntary action"; we call it the Automatic System.

Both these systems interact to produce our behavior, but a broad trend has been the growing recognition of the power of the Automatic System. However, psychology has viewed this trend very differently from economics. While economics has viewed the Automatic System in terms of deviations from "rational" decision making, many psychologists see the language of "bias" as flawed because they do not have an agreed standard model from which to deviate. Many of them stress that the Automatic System often produces better results. In fact, these differences have been the source of major debate.

Some researchers, led by the psychologist Gerd Gigerenzer, have claimed that the behavioral economics perspective is flawed because of its apparent focus on identifying and correcting biases. In their view, this focus denigrates people's ability to make good decisions. Instead they stress the power of heuristics and say that the key factor is whether such heuristics are well matched to the decision-making environment—in other words, whether there is "ecological rationality."[22] The best course of action for those trying to improve decision making is therefore to educate people on how to use heuristics effectively. The idea is that governments could help to "boost" people's ability to use the Automatic System, rather than just working round it.[23] In contrast, Daniel Kahneman is pessimistic about this kind of approach, precisely because we are not aware of when our Automatic System is guiding us.

The strength of a behavioral insights approach is that it can incorporate both perspectives. Sometimes the best option will be to design a policy that taps into the Automatic System to guide people toward particular options; at other times, it will be more effective to help people develop effective rules of thumb, like the food education examples in chapter 1. From the perspective of behavioral insights, the strength of evidence should inform which approach is taken—or how the options should be combined, since they are not mutually exclusive. This pragmatic and evidence-based nature of the behavioral insights approach is one of the reasons it has proven attractive to governments, as the last strand of our history makes clear.

## A Shift in How Governments Think about Behavior

Governments have always tried to understand and influence the behavior of those they govern, even if the role of the state has been the subject of fierce debate. In the seventeenth century, for example, Thomas Hobbes's landmark *Leviathan* tried to apply scientific principles to analyze how people interact in society, and to build an effective government based on the conclusions. As time went on, governments began to demand more sophisticated ways of understanding and addressing societal problems. In response, the twentieth century saw economists emerge as "technical experts whose advice is essential to decision making," and economics as the dominant mode of policy analysis.[24]

One reason for this change was that rational choice theory provided a clear process for understanding why people behaved as they did—and predicting how they were likely to act in response to government action. In other words, it helps governments get a grip on a problem. Take crime, for instance. If governments have only finite resources, how should they best use these to ensure levels of crime that voters find acceptable? In 1968, the economist Gary Becker said that the answer to this question was to "dispense with special theories of . . . [criminals'] psychological inadequacies" and instead "simply extend the economist's usual analysis of choice."[25] In other words, apply the principles of rational choice theory: people commit crimes if the benefits, as they see them, exceed the costs. Those costs can be summed up as the chance of being caught multiplied by the punishment given to someone who is caught.

The best government policies should therefore find the cheapest ways of increasing the costs to potential criminals. This basic insight can provide policymakers with a path to start generating policies. For example, one way of increasing the perceived chance of being caught may be to improve street lighting, so crimes become more visible. A recent real-world experiment tested this approach by randomly assigning public housing developments in New York City to receive streetlights or not. Increased visibility did seem to influence behavior. The researchers found that the streetlights led to at least a 36 percent reduction in nighttime outdoor "index crimes," which include offenses such as murder, robbery, and assault.[26] Policymakers can then conduct a "cost–benefit analysis" to determine whether this kind of result justifies the cost of providing the street lighting.

Finally, at a higher level, an economic perspective can provide a general framework to decide whether and when government should act at all. The rational actor model suggests that government intervention may be needed if there are "market failures," which can include monopolies (where too much power is concentrated in one market player), asymmetries of information (where one party in a transaction knows more than the other), or negative externalities (where an activity imposes costs on people outside the transaction, or on society at large—pollution being the best example). If these market failures occur, then the economic model also offers proposals for how governments respond, such as providing information to reduce asymmetries, taxation to redistribute wealth or to discourage actions with negative externalities, and regulation of activities if their social costs are seen to be too great.

Psychology found it hard to compete with this offer. It could not provide the same generally accepted, wide-ranging framework that produced clear results for policymakers. The US president had no Council of Psychological Advisers to sit alongside the Council of Economic Advisers set up in 1946, and most of the time, the people making policy followed Becker's advice to "dispense with" the theories of psychologists.

Of course, it's clearly not true that psychologists had zero input to policymaking, particularly for areas like transport, health, and the environment. For example, from the 1960s onward, many countries found that the traditional rational choice model was not helpful for increasing seatbelt usage, and instead drew on concepts from behavioral science, such as overconfidence and the importance of default settings, in order to gain results.[27] The practice of "social marketing" tried to improve societal outcomes by using social science to identify drivers of behavior that were not captured well in economic models. While social marketing saw popularity from the 1980s onward, it has usually occupied the secondary position of marketing a policy that has already been decided—by policymakers listening to economists.

However, this situation has started to change over the last fifteen or so years. Governments and policymakers have started to take a much greater interest in psychology and the behavioral sciences.[28] There are two main reasons for this shift: the first related to higher demand, and the second to an improved supply.

In terms of demand, there was a growing concern that the rational choice approach may have shortcomings. In some cases, policymakers were realizing that people were not behaving in line with the predictions of economic models. Take tax compliance. The main economic model for understanding tax compliance is based directly on Gary Becker's analysis of crime, already mentioned. In this model, the only factors that influence someone's tax behavior are the probability of audit, the size of fine or severity of punishment, tax rates, and income. The problem was that policymakers were getting data that did not seem to be in line with the model's predictions—other factors seemed to influence compliance as well. By 2007, one commentator could state that "empirical research consistently shows that the rational model is not working as neoclassical economists had intended."[29] In response, tax authorities have focused more on treating taxpayers like customers who need clear information, respect, and a competent service.

Policymakers may have paid particular attention to this kind of emerging data because the twenty-first century also saw renewed interest in evidence-based policymaking. Such an approach claims to be less interested in ideology, theory, or academic disciplines, since it is focused instead on finding out "What Works."[30] Therefore, if economic models no longer provide reliable predictions of what will work, policymakers may have been more willing to start looking around for better alternatives. The financial crisis of 2008 provided additional impetus. It showed that the existing economic approach to regulation had clearly failed, and organizations had behaved more in line with the updated "animal spirits" approach that behavioral economists had been developing. Moreover, in many countries it led to increased pressure on public finances that prompted policymakers to look for new approaches—ideally, inexpensive ones.

When they turned their eyes to other options, behavioral economics seemed an appealing prospect. As already noted, behavioral economics retained the familiar rational choice framework, but integrated new psychological findings as well (as deviations from that framework). Policymakers saw this as offering reliable explanations for some of the problems they had encountered, plus new tools for making better predictions in the future. At this point, behavioral economics may have seemed like a relatively unthreatening technical upgrade. Plus, as we are about to see, it also had some gifted advocates who could emphasize what was new, exciting, and intriguing about the approach.

So, at around the mid-2000s, our three strands of history come together: the rise of behavioral economics, the convergence on dual-process theories in psychology, and the growth of government interest in new accounts of human behavior. These created the conditions for the birth of behavioral insights.

## Nudge

At this promising point, Richard Thaler teamed up with the eminent legal scholar Cass Sunstein to develop a practical proposal for how governments could apply the evidence we have discussed so far. The result was the book *Nudge*, published in 2008. Thaler and Sunstein's basic argument was elegant and ingenious. People often use their Automatic System, which means their behavior deviates from rational choice theory. As the authors put it, we are "Humans not Econs." However, these deviations are predictable, and therefore policymakers can—and should—plan for them.

The first step is to understand how apparently unimportant features of the way choices are presented (the "choice architecture") can have a big influence on our decisions, since these features can trigger our mental shortcuts in response. Then, policymakers should design this "choice architecture" so that the Automatic System is likely to respond by preferring options that leave the person better off, as judged by that person. Crucially, persons are not forced to take this option; they should be free to choose a different option, if they want to. In other words, they are gently "nudged" toward one option or set of options, rather than being compelled to take them. Thaler and Sunstein are quite clear that a nudge must (a) not forbid any options; (b) not significantly change someone's economic incentives (e.g., by introducing substantive taxes or fines); and (c) be easy to avoid (i.e., should not impose other kinds of costs on a chooser). As they say: "Putting the fruit at eye level counts as a nudge. Banning junk food does not."

This food choice quote gives a flavor of the way the book is written—it is wry, punchy, conversational, and often irreverent. The first section presents a series of intriguing illusions and cognitive foibles and then explains why they occur. The following sections present examples of how these lessons could change the way we think about a range of problems concerning "health, wealth, and happiness." People are not saving enough for retirement? Change the default setting so that people are automatically enrolled into employer pension plans, rather than having to apply—and get them to commit to increasing their contribution rates when they get a pay raise in the future. Domestic energy use is increasing? Provide rapid feedback to consumers on how much energy they are using, and help them compare their usage with that of others.

Thaler and Sunstein were not just good at presentation; they also made smart choices when developing the concept of a nudge itself. Perhaps the most obvious is that nudging was carefully constructed to appeal to both the left and right of the political spectrum. In fact, Thaler and Sunstein came up with a new phrase to reflect this balance: "libertarian paternalism."[31] Nudging is paternalistic since it identifies a "best" choice (albeit to fulfill goals that individuals set themselves) and attempts to guide people toward that option. But it is libertarian because it does not remove options and acts gently: If people have a strong desire to choose differently, they can do so. In the eyes of the authors, this meant that nudging represented a "real third way" between left and right.

Other aspects of nudging proved persuasive as well. One argument that Thaler and Sunstein made forcefully is that there is no neutral design. Policymakers always have to make a decision about which options to present first, or to set what happens if someone does not make a choice at all. In other words, they are already "choice architects." In a cafeteria, there will always be some items that are more prominent than others, and therefore more likely to be chosen. Why let this positioning be determined simply by chance or custom? The logical conclusion is that everyone is in the business of nudging, whether they like it or not, and therefore they need to be aware of what they are doing.

Nudging also had the advantage of seeming to be cheap. Because it often focused on how an existing set of choices was arranged, there was the potential to achieve meaningful changes without major program spending. You just had to redesign an existing form or change the timing of an incentive (although, in truth, even these kinds of changes usually involve some kind of cost). As just noted, after 2008 this was music to the ears of cash-strapped policymakers.

However, stressing that nudges are cheap may also invite criticism that they can only scratch the surface of big issues. Since economic incentives and changes to legislation were off the table, how could nudging do enough heavy lifting to tackle ingrained societal problems? Thaler and Sunstein forestalled some of this criticism by tempering their claims. They do not claim that the nudges they propose are complete solutions to each problem they present. Instead, these are unexplored avenues that can bring tangible improvements at low cost. And Thaler and Sunstein freely admit that sometimes a nudge will not be enough.

The authors' efforts to make their ideas accessible, relevant, and acceptable paid off. The combination of accessible psychological insights and crunchy policy ideas tapped into the growing desire for alternatives to standard economic models. The result was that *Nudge* went on to sell more than 750,000 copies and was widely discussed in policy circles, where Thaler and Sunstein proved themselves persuasive advocates. Indeed, in 2009 Sunstein himself entered government as the head of the US Office of Information and Regulatory Affairs (OIRA), which focuses on regulation. Sunstein's mission was to apply behavioral economics to both increase the effectiveness of regulation and reduce the burdens it imposed.[32]

The high profile won by *Nudge* brought criticism as well, with the main charges being that nudging was manipulative, infantilizing, limited, overly individualistic, or based on inadequate evidence. We discuss these criticisms later. Another consequence was that nudging became fixed in many people's minds as the only way of applying behavioral science to policy, meaning that other approaches struggled to get traction. And despite the massive success, many policymakers still felt unsure about exactly how to apply these ideas in practice—there was a need for a more fleshed-out process that could be integrated into existing ways of doing things. We now explain how a set of developments in the UK came to answer that need and, in doing so, created a new approach for applying behavioral science to policy: behavioral insights.

MINDSPACE

Officials in the UK had shown a strong and growing interest in the behavioral sciences since at least the mid-1990s.[33] For example, in 2004 the Prime Minister's Strategy Unit published the report *Personal Responsibility and Changing Behaviour*, which discussed how many of the ideas we have just set out could be relevant to policy problems.[34] However, this report ran into trouble when a short speculative section on food pricing was turned into a front-page newspaper headline proclaiming "PM's Strategy Unit proposes fat tax."[35] A swift denial and rebuttal from the then Prime Minister meant that caution surrounded the application of behavioral science to policy for some years.

By 2009, after *Nudge*, there was renewed interest in returning to the topic, supported by the Head of the Civil Service, Gus O'Donnell. That year, the Labour government commissioned the think tank The Institute for Government to produce an official report on how behavioral science could be applied in practice. The team assembled for this task consisted of David Halpern (the lead author of the 2004 report), Paul Dolan (an economist), Ivo Vlaev (a cognitive psychologist), Dominic King (a surgeon working on behavioral economics), and one of us (Michael, then a senior researcher at the institute).

The report was to communicate the true scope of opportunity, in a way that compelled busy people to take the time to read it, and to feature real examples of credible policies informed by behavioral science. At its heart would be a simple mnemonic to help people remember the core points—and developing that mnemonic proved to be the central challenge. We had to identify the most reliable effects from behavioral science, while keeping the list short enough so it could be remembered easily. We were fortunate to identify the possibility of using the word "mind" early on. After much tweaking, this became MINDSPACE—with every letter standing for an effect that has a substantive influence on behavior (see figure 4).[36]

It is worth noting that MINDSPACE was not intended to be a comprehensively exhaustive, mutually exclusive academic framework. For example, some of these concepts focus on mental processes (salience, affect), while others focus more on ways of influencing those processes (defaults, incentives). But we were comfortable with making this trade-off because our main focus was on practical application, where these distinctions were less important. At the very least, we wanted busy policymakers to use MINDSPACE as a checklist to ensure they had taken these important factors into account.

MINDSPACE proved to be influential, being described later as "the intellectual foundation for the approach that was subsequently adopted [in the UK and elsewhere]"[37] and "of programmatic influence."[38] And, although this was not its main purpose, it also made an impact on academia

| Component | Description |
|---|---|
| Messenger | We are heavily influenced by who communicates information |
| Incentives | Our responses to incentives are shaped by predictable mental shortcuts, such as avoiding loss |
| Norms | We are strongly influenced by what others do |
| Defaults | We "go with the flow" of preset options |
| Salience | Our attention is drawn to things that seem novel and relevant |
| Priming | We can be influenced by cues we do not consciously notice |
| Affect | Emotional associations can shape our actions |
| Commitment | We seek to be consistent with our public promises and reciprocate favors |
| Ego | We act in ways that make us feel good about ourselves |

Figure 4

itself, being cited more than a thousand times since its publication. Some of this impact was probably due to the report's accessibility and innovative use of a mnemonic. But MINDSPACE also proved resilient because it recommended that behavioral science should have a wider role in policy than that set out in *Nudge*.

In strict terms, libertarian paternalism was only meant to help individuals fulfill their own goals. But what does it have to say about those instances where someone's goals harm others or society—with crime being the obvious example? Nudging also eschewed ruling out options or changing incentives—but what did that take off the table? MIND-SPACE addressed both those issues by considering the full range of policies and the full range of policy levers and arguing for the "integration of cultural, regulatory and individual change." Behavioral science should help officials understand the "behavioral dimension" of their policies and actions, rather than just focusing on new interventions. In this way, the report laid the foundations for the wider behavioral insights approach, which found its first expression when the Behavioural Insights Team was created six months later.

## The Behavioural Insights Team

It was not just the UK's bureaucracy or the ruling Labour Party who were becoming interested in the potential of behavioral science. True to *Nudge*'s unifying promise, the Conservative Party also became interested in the concept while in opposition, and Richard Thaler advised the party in the period before the 2010 UK general election.[39] In particular, the idea of nudging chimed with the desire by the center-right party to avoid legislation and instead use "insights from social psychology and behavioural economics to achieve our policy goals in a less burdensome and intrusive way."[40] When the party won power in 2010, this goal was included in the official Coalition Agreement that set the five-year agenda for the new administration.

During this period, the idea developed of creating a dedicated resource, in the center of government, to apply these concepts in a consistent, focused way. The result was the Behavioural Insights Team (BIT), a small team created as part of the Prime Minister's Office and the Cabinet Office. David Halpern was chosen as the head of the team, given his previous roles in government, and he gives a detailed account of BIT's birth and work in his book *Inside the Nudge Unit* (2015).[41] The following section is designed not to repeat that account but to show how the birth and growth of BIT catalyzed the adoption of behavioral insights: In our view, a couple of specific challenges that BIT faced ended up shaping the field of behavioral insights in important and enduring ways.

The context we want to highlight is that BIT was born into a fairly skeptical environment. There was strong support from the Prime Minister and the UK's most senior officials. However, many public officials suspected that the new administration had simply adopted the latest fashionable idea, possibly at the expense of more proven approaches. Many of them had seen high-profile teams set up at the center of government to implement a new approach, only to fizzle out with little done. They were also justifiably concerned that many of the findings that BIT would be applying might not work in real-world government contexts, as opposed to in laboratories.

Meanwhile, many sections of the media were also skeptical of the "Nudge Unit," as the team was universally called (partly because Thaler and Sunstein were generous enough to provide their support and expertise to BIT). At the start, the Nudge Unit was seen as a gimmicky invention that deserved faint ridicule through "nudge, nudge" jokes, or as a sinister endeavor to control the minds of the population without them realizing. A range of academics also voiced these concerns, plus others specific to their particular disciplines or political views.

BIT set about answering these concerns over several years. "In the end," as one academic observer put it, critics were "won over by the commonsense approach and the added value of such techniques."[42] But in the early days, this skepticism informed three important decisions: BIT's size, its sunset clause, and its commitment to evaluation.

First, BIT was created small: just seven people, partly to limit criticisms of unjustified spending at a time of squeezed government budgets. There had always been the intention that BIT would have aspects of a "skunk works"—a small group that develops radical ideas within a bureaucracy at low cost. But the lack of resources prompted a greater need to come up with innovative approaches (rather than just "throwing money at the problem"), while also requiring the team to be collaborative and persuasive, since it had to rely on partners to execute projects.

Second, BIT set up a "sunset clause": the team needed to demonstrate it had achieved three goals, and otherwise it was to be shut down on its second anniversary. This move was partly to inject a sense of urgency and momentum, while also creating a clear set of goals. They were to (1) transform at least two major areas of policy; (2) spread an understanding of behavioral approaches across the UK civil service; and (3) achieve at least a tenfold return on the cost of the team. Each of these goals was influential.

The first goal explicitly set the ambition that behavioral science should enter the "battleground of policy and strategy advice," rather than simply being about tweaking implementation.[43] Behavioral science should infuse core policy decisions, as economics had done, or it would be a footnote in history. The goal should be to maximize benefits to society and, as Richard Thaler puts it, to "nudge for good."

The second goal emphasized the importance of seeing behavioral insights as an approach, rather than just a collection of interesting ideas. Moreover, anyone—individuals and institutions—should be helped to apply this approach themselves, rather than it being the preserve of experts alone. The result was a commitment to openness: reports and toolkits were promoted widely, and access provided to the results of projects without charge.

The third goal meant the team often focused on less prominent or glamorous projects that nonetheless had a big financial impact, and thus were valued by administrators. These projects also had the advantage of often being quite uncontroversial, which reassured critics concerned about the team's potential activities. And often they could draw on large, reliable datasets, allowing results to be measured easily and reliably. These factors meant there was "low-hanging fruit" that produced "quick wins." A good example is BIT's extensive work to improve tax compliance through rewording the reminders sent to people who had not paid taxes on time. By getting into the system, modifying processes, and using existing data sources, BIT showed that hundreds of millions of pounds in revenue could be collected at low cost.

The third goal connects to a final, broader point. BIT also responded to skepticism by making sure its interventions were evaluated using the "gold standard" of randomized controlled trials (RCTs), discussed earlier and detailed in chapter 4. Using RCTs meant that the effects of a project could be reliably established and any benefits could be weighed against the costs incurred (which were often small). A decision could then be made on whether to adopt the change more widely, in a process BIT called "Test, Learn, Adapt."[44] Although many policymakers had not encountered this kind of experimental approach before, the trial results spoke to them in the familiar language of cost–benefit analysis that they knew from economists. The ability to convincingly show what difference a change had made began to bring increased credibility to the behavioral insights approach.

Increased credibility bred growing interest. Gradually, policymakers and administrators started to approach BIT with potential projects, rather than the other way around. Meeting this demand while continuing to innovate became difficult from within government, so BIT "spun out" in 2014 as a social purpose company. The organization is still partially owned by the UK government, which owns an equal share with the charity Nesta and the employees themselves. From 14 staff at spin-out, by 2020 the organization had grown to around 200 employees across seven offices globally and had conducted more than 500 randomized trials.

In sum: BIT's creation coined the term "behavioral insights," and then its activities developed a set of practices around this term (see chapter 4). Yet the story would be of

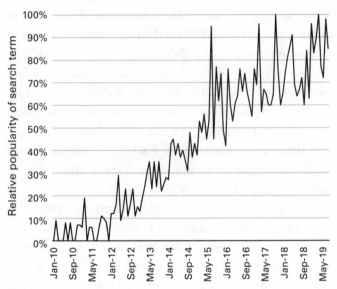

## Popularity of "Behavioral Insights" as a Search Term: 2010 to 2019

**Figure 5**

limited interest if it ended there. Instead, the concept and approach of behavioral insights began to spread to other governments and organizations around the world. Figure 5 gives a rough idea of the growing interest by displaying the trend in Google searches for the term "behavioural insights" (British spelling). By 2019, academic observers could note that "a new trend of 'Behavioral Insights' has entered the global policy scene."[45] BIT's work ended up acting as "a blueprint for the establishment of similar units elsewhere"[46] and became "a paradigmatic example for the translation of behavioural insights into public policy."[47]

## Behavioral Insights as a Movement

The behavioral insights movement advanced in several overlapping waves: initial copying of the BIT model; take-up and promotion by multilateral organizations; adoption by the private sector; and growth of a wider "ecosystem" that includes academia and individuals.

One wave consisted of creating "behavioral insights teams/units" modeled on BIT: a small, skilled group within the public sector that runs experiments and tries to influence policy. These became the "most typical organizational role model" for applying behavioral insights in government.[48] For example, various departments within the UK government (including revenue, work and pensions, health, and education) set up their own teams, which started to coalesce into a community that coordinated itself through a working group.

At the same time, BIT's results began to attract the attention of other governments, which started to set up their own dedicated teams. One high-profile example was the United States, which in 2013 started to quietly scope out a new Social and Behavioral Sciences Team (SBST). The team had a base in both the White House (the Office of Science and Technology Policy) and the Government Services Administration (the Office of Evaluation Sciences). The team focused particularly on low-cost, measurable interventions like increasing vaccine uptake, raising retirement savings rates, and boosting college enrollment.[49] But it also dealt with more complex policy challenges, such as the contamination of drinking water in the city of Flint, Michigan.

The success of the SBST was reflected by the issuing in 2015 of Executive Order 13707, "Using behavioral science insights to better serve the American people." On the basis that "by improving the effectiveness and efficiency of Government, behavioral science insights can support a range of national priorities," the Executive Order directed departments and agencies to apply these insights in practice, and to recruit experts in behavioral science. The White House element of the team was disbanded after the inauguration of Donald Trump. However, the Office of Evaluation Sciences continues its work of running RCTs informed by behavioral science, which showed the wisdom of originally splitting the team between a political base and an administrative base.

In very rough terms, this first wave of adoption lasted until around 2014, at which point at least 51 countries had created a centrally directed behavioral insights program.[50] Then, high-profile multilateral organizations gave the approach another push. Major reports from the World Bank (2015), the OECD (2015 and 2017), the European Commission (2016), and the United Nations (2017) backed behavioral insights as an important new approach—some going far as calling it a "paradigm shift" in public administration.[51] And these reports were backed up by action. Each of these organizations set up its own units or teams dedicated to applying behavioral insights to advance institutional goals (e.g., the European Commission's "Foresight and Behavioural Insights Unit"). The emphasis on evidence and evaluation in the field of behavioral insights was clearly attractive to these actors, which are united by a technocratic drive to improve how government works.

Support from these kinds of organizations lent more legitimacy to behavioral insights, making the approach seem even more like a promising practice that should be tried at least once by a government. And so more countries followed, with the most recent being India, which began setting up a central "nudge unit" in September 2019. According to the OECD, 202 public entities around the world were applying behavioral insights to their work by November 2018. As a result, "behavioral insights can no longer be seen as a fashionable short-term foray by public bodies. They have taken root in many ways across many countries around the world and across a wide range of sectors and policy areas."[52]

When looking at the growth of these units, a few points are worth making. This was not a trend for economically developed countries only: Many developing countries in Africa, South America, and Asia took up the approach. While the BIT model of a leading central unit was perhaps the most prevalent, several other setups were tried. For example, the Netherlands never established a centralized presence, but rather had distributed experts who were brought together in knowledge networks and working groups. And it was not just national governments that made these changes: Teams were also established at the local, regional, and subnational levels, like the Behavioural Insights Group in the Canadian province of British Columbia.

Finally, not all these initiatives were successful. Quite a lot of different elements were needed, plus some luck. Political support was a crucial factor, even if it just provided "cover," rather than active encouragement. Buy-in from administrative leaders was possibly even more important. Team members needed to possess technical expertise, in terms of both behavioral science and evaluation techniques. At the same time, they needed to be persuasive, to be pragmatic, and to understand how to get things done in bureaucracies. Officials who had both knowledge and a practical edge were often not easy to find.

## A Behavioral Insights "Ecosystem" Emerges

On the face of it, the private sector was slower to embrace behavioral insights. The truth is that commercial organizations had been using different aspects of behavioral insights; they just had not reaped the benefits of combining them.

On one hand, there was a long history of companies using psychology to market their products.[53] Back in 1957, Vance Packard's wildly popular *Hidden Persuaders* argued that businesses were using widespread psychological manipulation to drive sales (although their approach was quite different from dual-process theories). On the other hand, the private sector was no stranger to running randomized experiments or, as they often call them, "A/B tests." Experiments with direct mailings had been going on for decades—back in 2000, the credit card company Capital One ran 60,000 RCTs that year.[54] (However, we also need to be careful not to overstate the prevalence of A/B testing in the private sector. A recent study shows that only 8 to 17 percent of startups use A/B testing technology, for example.)[55] The issue is that these two practices often remained separate. The applications of psychology were not always tested robustly, while the robust tests often lacked structure and theory—and instead "threw things at a wall to see what sticks." The result was that it was difficult to build on previous findings consistently.

As the private sector began to look at behavioral insights—particularly as popularized in books like *Nudge*—several advantages came into focus. Dual-process theories offered an organizing framework that was simple enough to be easily used and understood, while still providing useful predictions about human behavior. The experiments were convincing and "scientific," but also offered intriguing and unexpected ideas about "what makes people tick." And the shift to digital environments meant that companies had new, rapidly expanding arenas for conducting their own tests—and discovering what return on investment was possible.

The result was an explosion of firms offering behavioral insights for business. These could be specialized, boutique consultancies or new functions within established firms. Compared with public-sector teams, they tended to place greater emphasis on "combining a scientific understanding of behavior with the power of creativity," in the words of Ogilvy & Mather's Ogilvy Change practice. Some large companies—like AIG, Google, Amazon, Walmart, and Johnson & Johnson—decided to create their own dedicated teams. Others hired "Chief Behavioral Officers" to ensure that evidence about human behavior was built into strategic conversations at the highest level, rather than being an afterthought.

This last point reflects that companies were not just looking to maximize sales. They also saw the potential for using behavioral insights to reshape the way organizations worked. Processes and norms could be reengineered to help employees become healthier and work more efficiently.[56] In the boardroom, executives turned to behavioral science to reduce discrimination by race and gender,[57] while management consultancies touted the benefits of "behavioral strategy" that avoided common cognitive biases. Businesses also saw the need to "nudge for good" as well, since sometimes public and private goals align. For example, pilots with Virgin Atlantic adopted more fuel-efficient flying procedures after academics developed timely, targeted feedback and monitoring interventions. The company saved money and increased employees' job satisfaction, but also prevented nearly 25,000 tons of carbon dioxide from entering the atmosphere.[58]

Of course, many criticisms could be made here. Often private-sector practitioners were not subject to the same level of scrutiny as those in the public sector, since the drivers for transparency were weaker. Many in the field of advertising and marketing would admit that they struggled to instill a culture of robustly evaluating consumer behaviors. And some of those behaviors being encouraged may have downsides for the targeted individuals.

Increasingly, issues like these were being discussed in networks of practitioners and thinkers on the topic. Academics began to engage more with the practical and political issues created by applying behavioral science in practice, as well as advancing that science itself. Harvard University set up a "Behavioral Insights Group" to create experts of the future; the new Behavioral Science & Policy Association connected the current ones, as did a rash of new international conferences; journals such as *Behavioural Public Policy* and the *Journal of Behavioral Public Administration* were created to chart and critique these changes.

One final group in this emerging behavioral insights ecosystem cannot be neglected: nonexperts. As we mentioned in the context of food education, individuals and informal groups can take the insights from behavioral science and use them to accomplish their own goals more effectively.[59] For example, many people feel anxious before they need to perform a task like speaking in public or participating in an important meeting. Most people try a strategy of trying to calm down in order to deal with this anxiety. But an alternative approach is to reinterpret this anxiety as excitement. A study found that when people use this tactic they perform better at anxiety-inducing tasks.[60] This is the kind of useful yet easy tactic, informed by behavioral science, that people can apply to their everyday lives.

We have now traced the history of behavioral insights from the assembling of its academic foundations to the growth of an ecosystem of many actors, priorities, opportunities, and tensions. But in any history, the drive to keep the narrative going means things are missed. In the next chapter, we want to dwell on some examples that we think bring home what a behavioral insights approach is, and what it can do.

# EXAMPLES OF BEHAVIORAL INSIGHTS IN PRACTICE

Now that we've defined the behavioral insights approach and charted its history, this chapter aims to give a better sense of its application to real-world problems. To do this we give a handful of concise examples that vary by place and issue. We seek to contrast each example with more common approaches to solving these sorts of problems.

The examples are organized by a simple framework for different kinds of interventions. This framework starts with the three basic categories of intervention that featured in figure 2: rules, incentives, and information. We give examples of how each of these interventions can be enhanced through behavioral insights. To these, we add two other categories that are important but often neglected: interventions that change processes or the decision environment. This framework is not exhaustive, but we think that it is useful.

Here and elsewhere in the book, we discuss many of the concepts within behavioral insights (e.g., defaults, social norms, framing effects). However, we will not cover every one of these ideas and their effects on behavior; this guide is not comprehensive, but rather offers the essentials. We offer a definition of many of these ideas in the glossary.

## Rules: Green by Default

Switching to a greener household energy plan is one way that many of us could reduce our carbon emissions. Traditional approaches to increasing switching usually involve giving us more or different information to influence our decision. Switching rates remain low, though; energy can be a difficult market to shop and the perceived hassle of doing so is high. In Germany, in the late 1990s, an energy company broadened its service to include three plans: the cheapest and least environmentally friendly one; a mid-priced but greener plan; and one that was more expensive but even more eco-friendly. Since customers had to be on one of the three plans, the starting point—the preselected default—was the mid-priced option. Customers had to actively respond to the letter if they wanted to switch to either of the other two plans.

To highlight the rule change, 150,000 letters were mailed out informing customers that they could choose any of the three plans, but that doing nothing would keep them on the preselected mid-priced option. As you might expect from what you have already read, the results were striking: After two months, 94 percent of customers stuck with the default plan,[1] with the effect of automatically flipping most of a market to a greener alternative overnight. Just 4.3 percent went with the cheaper option, 1 percent chose the greenest but more expensive plan, and 0.7 percent of customers switched to another supplier. It is not just consumers who are influenced by defaults: 80 percent of countries accept treaty adjudication by the International Court of Justice when it is the default option, compared with only 5 percent when the country has to actively choose it.[2]

Changing system-level laws or rules is not always possible. However, we can also try to improve the rules of thumb individuals use for making decisions. For example, teaching credit-card customers to replace their existing decision processes with a simple rule of thumb—use cash if the purchase is under $20—led to an average reduction of $104 in revolving debt six months later compared to a control group.[3] Or entrepreneurs can be taught simple, reliable rules of thumb to help them follow basic accounting practices—such as calculating business profits by physically separating business and personal accounts into drawers, with a simple rule about transferring between the two. An RCT found that this approach improved financial management by around ten percentage points, compared to standard accounting training.[4]

## Incentives: When Nonfinancial Rewards Are Better Than Money

In 2010, Zambia's adult HIV prevalence was 14.3 percent—one of the highest rates in the world—but demand for protective contraception was low. To promote the use of contraception, researchers led by Nava Ashraf recruited influential messengers—specifically, hairdressers and barbers—to sell female condoms. Since resources are typically limited, it was important to test whether monetary rewards would be necessary to ensure that the messengers participated or whether nonfinancial incentives might suffice. The stylists were randomized to receive one of the following: a 90 percent commission on sales; a 10 percent commission; a nonfinancial incentive, consisting of a public progress chart that documented sales and emphasized the contribution sales make to the overall health goal; or a volunteer "contract" and no reward (the control group). The condom sales of the groups were then monitored.

While the financial incentives were no more effective overall than the control, over the course of a year the sellers with the progress chart sold more than twice the number of condoms than any other group. These results hold true for at least a year, so they are not just driven by novelty. The design of the experiment allowed the researchers to show that the progress chart worked by increasing the effort expended by the messengers, rather than by increasing demand from consumers. Had all stylists been offered nonfinancial incentives, they would have sold 22,496 condoms: 11,810 more condoms than if they had all been volunteers.[5] The results of this experiment show that applying behavioral insights to incentives, such as incorporating public signals of success and outcome-oriented progression charts, can increase motivation in low-resource environments, even outperforming traditional financial incentives.

Financial incentives are undoubtedly a powerful influence on behavior. However, as suggested in chapter 1, behavioral insights can also be used to design them in more effective ways. For example, in one study giving financial rewards for group outcomes resulted in greater healthy weight loss compared with rewarding individual performance: the added motivation to not let down a teammate supercharged the promise of financial gain.[6]

## Information: The Effect of Who Says What, and How They Say It

Many of the best-known examples of behavioral insights concern changing the framing of information related to a decision. For example, many tax authorities around the world have run experiments showing that changing the presentation of forms or reminder letters can substantially increase tax compliance. These changes might involve introducing new information, such as stating that the recipient is in the minority of people who have not paid, or they can focus on making existing information clearer, like clarifying exactly what someone is required to do in a particular situation.[7] While these kind of general effects of a message on a whole population matter, we should also consider how specific subgroups react. For example, research by Elizabeth Linos shows that job advertisements highlighting the challenging nature of police work are more effective at attracting applicants than those that take the more traditional approach of focusing on public protection and service. But in addition to this overall difference in effectiveness, the "challenge" message is three times as effective for people of color and women applicants.[8] We say more on this point in the final chapter.

Just as changing a message's presentation can affect results, so too can changing the messenger. For example, a series of studies in the United States compared the effect of a motivational message from a beneficiary of a worker's efforts to the same message from their team leader. These studies found that when emphasizing the positive impact of a task, beneficiaries were significantly more effective than leaders when it comes to improving productivity and performance.[9] Similar messenger effects have been found in charitable giving,[10] smoking cessation,[11] and promoting agreement with court rulings.[12] Finally, the timing of a message matters more than we often realize. Prompting drivers to wear seatbelts immediately before driving increases seatbelt use, while reminding them five minutes beforehand does not.[13]

## Environment: Improving Workplace Safety by Redesigning the Floor Space around Workstations

Globally, there are an estimated 340 million workplace accidents each year.[14] These accidents are enormously damaging to both individuals' lives and their contribution to the economy. While some accidents are a result of poor working conditions, others stem from the behavior of workers. For example, employees in a Chinese textile factory were in the habit of throwing waste scraps of cloth on the floor next to them, creating a slipping hazard. An explanation of why this habit had formed was that workers were financially motivated to continue working without breaks. Initially, the factory tried a traditional approach to influence behavior: offering monetary incentives to workers if they put waste in trash cans. The effect was disappointing: scraps were still thrown on the floor, and the danger remained.

Sherry Jueyu Wu and Betsy Levy Paluck, researchers partnering with the factory, thought that meaningful visual cues on the floor might help change behavior. Specifically, they introduced decals depicting golden coins on the production floors. Culturally, golden coins are considered to symbolize fortune and luck, meaning the employees would have a disincentive to cover them with waste. Introducing these decals led to a 20 percent decline in waste on the floor.[15] A small, contextually meaningful change to the design of the environment was enough to overcome a seemingly entrenched habit.

### Process: Making Colonoscopies More Bearable by Exploiting the Peak-End Effect

Received wisdom in medicine is that it's "better to get it over with." This ethos, coupled with efficiency considerations, means that speed is often implicitly valued in medical procedures, especially where pain is involved. In 1995, a team of physicians and academics based in Toronto was grappling with a very specific research problem: decreasing pain perception among colonoscopy patients. Their research hinged on a phenomenon known as the "peak-end rule." This rule states that our judgment and memory is disproportionately shaped by the peak moment and the very last part of an experience. Since colonoscopies at the time typically conformed to the notion of "better to get it over with," they inevitably induced significant discomfort in the final moments. A slower "exit," the team hypothesized, would be perceived as less unpleasant, even though it would make for a longer procedure. The insight proved correct: patients whose colonoscopies involved an additional three minutes of slow extraction rated their overall pain to be lower and had a more favorable view of the experience.[16]

These brief examples show that behavioral insights can have a substantial effect on important issues. They do not, however, shed light on how these interventions are designed or the effects measured. In the next chapter we turn our attention to the practical steps of applying behavioral insights.

# APPLYING BEHAVIORAL INSIGHTS

There is no shortage of guides that propose how behavioral insights should be applied in practice. Most include a common set of principles and activities to identify the behavioral dimensions of problems, devise potential solutions, and evaluate their impact. This chapter gives a succinct account of these core features, rather than offering a complete "how to" guide. Our focus on essential knowledge means that we do not review all the relevant literature or give detailed explanations of how to conduct site visits. A useful starting point for a more in-depth treatment is the OECD's BASIC toolkit.[1]

To structure this account, we will walk through some work that Elspeth did on job seeking. This project was developed with a UK unemployment center (Bedford Jobcentre) and focused on increasing attendance at recruitment events by those looking for work. We tested whether attendance could be influenced by changing the wording of a standard text (SMS) invitation sent to prospective attendees. As it turned out, the message that performed the best more than doubled attendance.

We chose this example because it was a fairly straightforward piece of work, making it easy to draw out the key lessons. It also fits within a larger policy area—reducing unemployment—which means we can zoom out and show the wider context at key moments. Finally, the project has also been published in an academic journal, where readers can learn more about it in more depth.[2]

This chapter presents ten steps:

1.  Establish the scope.

2.  Break the challenge into addressable parts.

3.  Identify the target outcome.

4.  Map the relevant behaviors.

5.  Identify the factors that affect each behavior.

6.  Choose the priority behaviors to address.

7.  Create evidence-led intervention(s).

8.  Implement the intervention(s).

9.  Assess the effects.

10. Take further action based on the results.

We present this process as linear in order to make it clear. In reality, there are feedback loops between these stages, as we revisit previous decisions in the light of new knowledge. We flag where those iterations are likely to occur.

## Step 1: Establish the Scope

We start with the big picture: the overall goal of the work. In this example, that overall goal is to reduce unemployment. We recognize that starting with the overall goal is a top-down approach; it could be possible to begin at a micro level, looking at individual behaviors and working out goals from that level up. In those cases, we would move more quickly through these initial scoping steps.

With the overall goal in mind, we then need to identify whether we are approaching this goal at a tactical or strategic level. As we discussed in chapter 1, some projects are tactical, dealing with changes at an operational level or within only a limited part of a system. Others allow for intervention at a more strategic level, opening up opportunities to alter the fundamental policy or structures for addressing an issue, and perhaps changing a whole system. While the exact opportunities are unlikely to be clear at this stage, we want to make this judgment because using behavioral insights is a pragmatic approach: we do not want to spend a lot of time pursuing options that are not "on the table."

One way of establishing the scope is to identify the kinds of interventions that are likely to be feasible. To do this, we suggest five questions, based on the framework from chapter 3, that help to define the parameters of the work more tightly. These questions may be easier to answer in parallel with completing Step 2. The questions are:

1. Can you change the fundamental *rules* that govern the system, such as regulations, laws, or policies?

2. Can you change the *incentives* that motivate action, such as the social or economic costs and benefits of certain behaviors?

3. Can you change the *information* provided?

4. Can you change the *environment* in which decisions are made (e.g., the space in which certain activities are completed)?

5. Can you change the *process* actors go through, for example, removing or reducing barriers to progress?

In the example we follow through this chapter, the scope was clearly in the tactical realm because the work had to be completed quickly, without additional resources, and in one individual employment center within a larger system. The modes of intervention were also constrained since the commissioning partner only had control over the employment center processes, environment, and information. By determining these factors up front, we were able to focus during Steps 2 through 6 on identifying elements of the problem where the desired behaviors could be achieved with the interventions available.

The tactical nature and constrained scope of this example allow us to give a clear and clean account of the process. A tactical example is also likely to have the widest applicability. We have found that most organizations have at least some tactical opportunities to apply behavioral insights quickly and effectively; in contrast, opportunities for strategic interventions tend to vary more by context (e.g., only governments can regulate). Nevertheless, in Step 10 we also consider an example from our broader work on labor markets where the scope was strategic in nature and most modes of intervention were possible. In cases like this, Steps 2 and 3 are likely to take much longer because they are essential to narrowing the focus.

*Result of this step*: We confirmed that this work was tactical in scope, and interventions would likely be limited to changing the information, environment, or processes in the unemployment center we are working with.

## Step 2: Break the Challenge into Addressable Parts

Behavioral insights may be applied to problems that are complex, sprawling, and produced or solved by many actors. In order to achieve the overall goal of reducing unemployment, we first need to identify the basic conditions for achieving that goal and the actors and actions that generate those conditions. A simplified example of this unpacking process is shown in figure 6, which should be read from left to right.

By getting more specific about who does what, we can better assess the opportunities for intervention. For example, as shown in figure 6, only a few actions can be initiated by any individual unemployed person. On the other hand, national governments can make wide-ranging structural changes to employment law, the benefits they offer to those out of work, or the regulations businesses follow when hiring. While behavioral insights can complement such changes, they are often slow, expensive, and politically loaded. Compare this to an individual unemployment center trying a new way of communicating what skills the local labor market needs, or an employer tweaking its application process to prevent its recruiters from introducing bias. The possible changes vary greatly in terms of their expected impact and feasibility.

We can then apply the limited scope established in Step 1 to see that by focusing on unemployment center

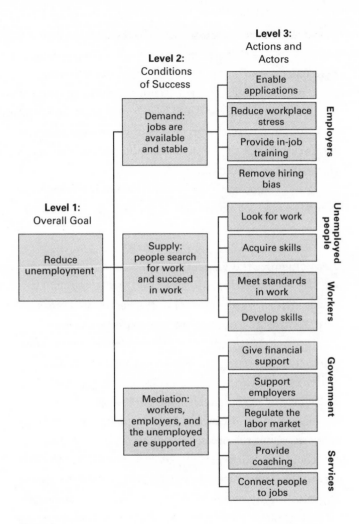

**Level 1:**
Overall Goal

**Level 2:**
Conditions
of Success

**Level 3:**
Actions and
Actors

Reduce
unemployment

Demand:
jobs are
available
and stable

Enable
applications

Reduce workplace
stress

Provide in-job
training

Remove hiring
bias

Employers

Supply:
people search
for work
and succeed
in work

Look for work

Acquire skills

Unemployed
people

Meet standards
in work

Develop skills

Workers

Mediation:
workers,
employers, and
the unemployed
are supported

Give financial
support

Support
employers

Regulate the
labor market

Government

Provide
coaching

Connect people
to jobs

Services

Figure 6

processes, we are operating in the bottom right-hand corner of figure 6. We then assessed which opportunities were most promising in terms of feasibility and likely impact on the overall goal. We discuss these impact and feasibility criteria in more detail later, since they are useful at various stages of the process. Our conclusion was that better connecting of people to available jobs was the most promising opportunity.

*Result of this step*: We chose to focus on the way in which the unemployment center connected people to jobs.

## Step 3: Identify the Target Outcome

In this step we need to work out the best way to measure progress toward reducing unemployment, based on our scoping in Steps 1 and 2, the data available, and the time scale we are operating on. In this case, since we focused on how the unemployment center connects people to jobs, we needed to find a reasonable measure of that action.

Unemployment centers connect jobseekers to jobs in many ways, but the project team's analysis suggested that one route was particularly promising: mass-recruitment events. These were events put on by the unemployment center in partnership with a local employer (a new supermarket or factory, for example) that needed to fill many vacant roles quickly. The events tended to be successful at getting people into work, and therefore the center invested in developing relationships with employers, staffing the events, and coaching its clients during applications. Ensuring that jobseekers attend the events in the first place is obviously crucial. Prior to the event, the unemployment center identified which candidates were eligible and sent them an SMS invitation to attend. However, despite the high likelihood of getting a job, only around 10 percent of eligible applicants typically attended.

The rate of attendance at mass-recruitment events among invited jobseekers had several features that made it a good target outcome. Attendance was a behavior that had a clear link to the overall goal, since the events were often effective at helping people into work. This target outcome was also relatively specific: the group involved was well defined and there was consensus on how attendance was defined and measured. (For some outcomes, we may also define the time period during which we aim to achieve the target outcome.) Moreover, the desired behavior was already being reliably recorded by existing systems, minimizing costs and uncertainty. Finally, achieving movement in the target outcome seemed possible. Not only was the existing rate of attendance low, evidence indicated that most jobseekers were motivated to find work, making it plausible that relatively small changes (say, making it marginally easier to attend) could harness this motivation and result in change.

Building on this point, the next step is to determine how much change in the target outcome would constitute success. The parties involved in the intervention need to agree early on a "good enough" improvement. At its simplest, this can be a question of cost–benefit analysis: what level of improvement would justify the budget available for an intervention? However, often the aspiration is greater than this basic requirement. In unemployment policy, for example, many governments have highly ambitious targets for national employment levels that far exceed the threshold at which benefits surpass costs.

But what aspirations are realistic? To answer this question we need to consider the existing evidence. For example, if the ambition is to increase local employment rates by 10 percent, yet the most effective existing interventions only achieve a 1 percent increase, then expectations should be readjusted or the project reconsidered. By setting these expectations early, we provide an anchor point for each step of the process: a way to check back against the original ambition.

For this project, we collectively determined that moving from 10 percent to 15 percent invitee attendance (that is, a 50 percent increase) would be a reasonable target. Such an increase struck a balance between what was needed to justify the investment of effort and what, based on a review of similar interventions, we considered to be a realistic change. This target became more specific as we gained more information, but the basics remained stable.

*Result of this step*: Our target outcome is to increase the rate of attendance at mass-recruitment events among invited jobseekers from 10 percent to 15 percent.


## Step 4: Map the Relevant Behaviors

Now we need to understand what behaviors produce the outcome (attendance at recruitment events). In this case, that means gathering more information about the recruitment events in question, how they come about, how jobseekers are made aware of them, and any other relevant contextual information. The tools for finding this information include reviewing previous research on the topic; using qualitative research approaches such as interviews, observations, focus groups, and experiencing the process firsthand; and employing quantitative methods such as surveys and data analysis. As noted, we cannot explain these tools in depth here.

We need to consider the strengths and weaknesses of each tool and where the gaps in our understanding are. For example, if we already have some initial conclusions about user experience based on the feedback about a service, we might seek to validate those conclusions by direct observations and by cross-referencing the feedback with administrative data about how the service is being used. Cross-referencing is important because feedback alone can only tell us some of the story: it may disproportionately represent those who had a particularly good or bad experience. Direct observation can reveal new aspects of user experience, while administrative data can tell us whether patterns we see in the feedback (such as long wait times) are representative of users in general. Together, this information can give us a more reliable picture of what is happening.

To map the relevant behaviors in Bedford, we conducted brief interviews, observations of how people were using the center, and reviews of documents that guide operations. The goal was to map the relevant behaviors from the perspective of the jobseeker and the unemployment center, identify who is (perceived to be) involved by each party, and identify any fundamental differences in experience or perspective. Through this process we identified four groups influencing the outcome: (1) unemployed people (jobseekers), (2) unemployment center staff, (3) prospective employers, and (4) the social support network (typically friends and family) surrounding the unemployed person.

Each group could perform a specific set of behaviors to increase the likelihood of a jobseeker attending the recruitment event. The diagram in figure 7 shows the relevant behaviors in a swimlane diagram, a common form

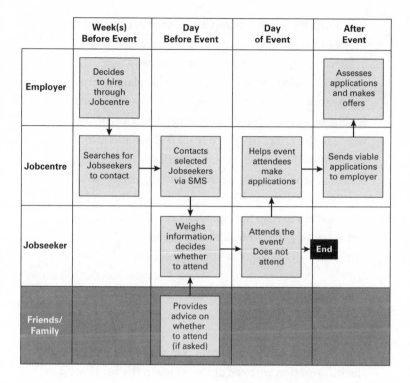

| | Week(s) Before Event | Day Before Event | Day of Event | After Event |
|---|---|---|---|---|
| **Employer** | Decides to hire through Jobcentre | | | Assesses applications and makes offers |
| **Jobcentre** | Searches for Jobseekers to contact | Contacts selected Jobseekers via SMS | Helps event attendees make applications | Sends viable applications to employer |
| **Jobseeker** | | Weighs information, decides whether to attend | Attends the event/ Does not attend | End |
| **Friends/ Family** | | Provides advice on whether to attend (if asked) | | |

Figure 7

of process map in which each group has its own "lane" or row and the process is laid out horizontally, showing the handoffs between groups at each step.

In this case, we found a good degree of consistency on the perceived behaviors from both sides, with the exception that some jobseekers listed friends and family as being involved—this group was invisible from the unemployment center perspective.

By laying out the behaviors this way, we can focus on who is doing what and their likely relative impact on the overall outcome. For example, whether the invitation is sent or not will have a very large effect on attendance, whereas the effect of advice from friends and family may be smaller. The behaviors that contribute to the target outcome are labeled by numbered diamonds in figure 8.

*Result of this step*: We brought together the exploratory information to map the behaviors relevant to attending or not attending mass-recruitment events.

### Step 5: Identify the Factors That Affect Each Behavior

In order to influence these behaviors, we need to understand what is producing them. We may have gathered all the information we need at this stage in the previous step, but sometimes this exercise can reveal unresolved questions. In these cases, we might conduct further exploratory research.

So, how can we identify the factors underlying these behaviors? One useful model is the COM-B model, which organizes the factors that produce behavior into three main categories:

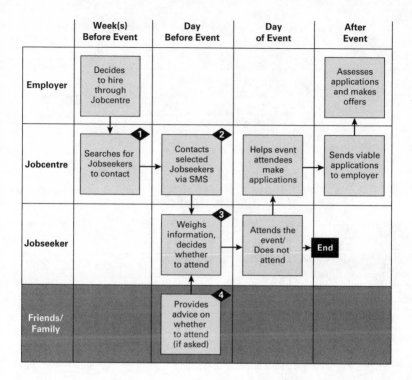

|  | Week(s) Before Event | Day Before Event | Day of Event | After Event |
|---|---|---|---|---|
| **Employer** | Decides to hire through Jobcentre | | | Assesses applications and makes offers |
| **Jobcentre** | Searches for Jobseekers to contact ❶ | Contacts selected Jobseekers via SMS ❷ | Helps event attendees make applications | Sends viable applications to employer |
| **Jobseeker** | | Weighs information, decides whether to attend ❸ | Attends the event/ Does not attend → End | |
| **Friends/ Family** | | Provides advice on whether to attend (if asked) ❹ | | |

Figure 8

1. *Capability*: the individual's psychological and physical capacity to engage in the activity concerned, including having the right skills and knowledge.

2. *Opportunity*: factors outside the control of the individual that enable or prompt a behavior.

In order to influence behaviors, we need to understand what is producing them.

3. *Motivation*: cognitive processes that drive the behavior, including both conscious and nonconscious decision making, habit, and emotional responses.[3]

Figure 9 shows a simplified version of the analysis of influencing factors for this project.

As mentioned in previous chapters, the behavioral insights approach does not have to be individualistic. A concrete way to think about this point at this stage is that opportunity factors (which fall outside the control of the individual actor) can be used as points for intervention. To develop an intervention we must now use the lessons from this stage to rank each behavior based on how easy it

| Behavior | Description | Contributing factors |
|---|---|---|
| 1 | Choose who gets invited to the event | • Capability: ability to classify skills<br>• Opportunity: number of jobs available (determines if filter is strict or not); the structure of the official occupation classification. |
| 2 | Construct and send invites | • Opportunity: timing of message is usually opportunistic due to busy schedule.<br>• Motivation: staff prefer to minimize effort (use default template and mode of communication). |
| 3 | Make decision on whether to attend event | • Opportunity: may have preexisting plans at attendance time;<br>• Motivation: perceived chance of being hired; weighting of advice from others; low morale and low self-efficacy; inattention |
| 4 | Provide advice on whether to attend | • Opportunity: may not know about the event.<br>• Capability: may not have a good sense of the labor market and cannot, therefore, give good advice on the quality of the prospective job. |

Figure 9

is to change, and how much impact that any such change would create.

*Result of this step*: We uncovered the factors that influence the relevant behaviors, identifying barriers and enablers.

## Step 6: Choose Priority Behaviors to Address

This is the final step before we can create interventions to improve attendance at recruitment events (in service of the larger goal to reduce unemployment). For each behavior identified, we assign a rank based on the expected impact from making a change and the feasibility of doing so, using prompting questions like these:

1. Impact: How important is this behavior to the outcome?

    a. Is this behavior on the critical path to the outcome? In other words, to what extent does it influence attendance at the recruitment event?

    b. How many people enact this behavior? How many do not?

2. Feasibility: How likely is it that this behavior can be changed?

a. Can we modify any of the factors influencing the behavior?

b. Would the required changes be politically palatable? Are they likely to be affordable? Could they be accomplished in the available time frame?

c. Are there other demands, in terms of either time or resources, on the relevant individual or organization that will make changing this behavior difficult?

These questions are deliberately general and at a high level; in reality, the ranking is informed by additional factors and depends on context. The conclusion of this assessment in Bedford was that we should focus on two interrelated behaviors identified in figure 9:

• 2: A Bedford Jobcentre staffer constructs and sends the invitation (British, "the invite") to the event via SMS.

• 3: On receiving the SMS, the recipient decides whether to attend the event.

Specifically, this ranking identifies the factors relating to "motivation" in each of these behaviors to be both malleable and impactful in improving the overall outcome. Figure 10 gives a simple visual representation of the ranking results.

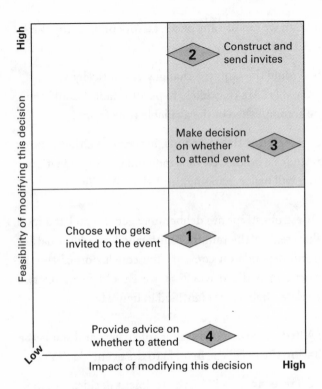

High

Feasibility of modifying this decision

Low

Impact of modifying this decision    High

2  Construct and send invites

3  Make decision on whether to attend event

1  Choose who gets invited to the event

4  Provide advice on whether to attend

Figure 10

*Result of this step*: We identified two priority behaviors to target with the intervention: the construction and sending of the SMS invitation; and determining whether to attend the event.

## Step 7: Create Evidence-Led Interventions to Produce the Priority Behaviors

By the end of this seventh step, we will have a proposed intervention that should result in the priority behavior(s) we have identified. First, we need to specify the solution requirements based on the factors that we know will influence the behavior. Figure 11 shows how this was done in Bedford. The influencing factors in gray are considered out of scope because changing them was not judged to be feasible. The ones in black, meanwhile, need to be addressed by our solution. To identify the specific solution requirements, we conducted a literature review looking at how barriers and enablers similar to those identified in the COM-B exercise have been overcome or exploited in other projects. In this case, our search focused on how to attract attention and make mass messaging feel personal; how to change perceptions of the likelihood of getting a job; and how to prompt action in the face of low morale.

To meet the requirements associated with devising and sending the message, we chose to test whether varying

| Behavior | Contributing factors | Solution requirement |
|---|---|---|
| **2** Construct and send invites | Opportunity: timing of message is usually opportunistic due to busy schedule. Motivation: staff prefer to minimize effort (use default template and mode of communication). | • Harness status quo bias and effort aversion: use existing communication channels, processes, automation, and templates were possible. |
| **3** Make decision on whether to attend event | Opportunity: may have preexisting plans at attendance time. Motivation: • perceived chance of being hired; • weighting of advice from others; • low morale and low self-efficacy; • inattention. | • Use personalization to attract attention and increase the perception that this is a tailored opportunity. • Evoke positive emotional affect to overcome low morale with a personalized and caring message. |

Figure 11

the wording of existing SMS invitations would increase attendance. To select this intervention, we again applied the criteria of impact and feasibility, but added two additional considerations: acceptability and scalability. Acceptability concerns whether there are political or ethical issues with a proposed intervention (we discuss this issue in depth in the next chapter). Scalability concerns whether the intervention could be used beyond an initial pilot or test site. For example, we made sure that—if successful—the message that performed best could replace the existing default template in the national system. While this requirement increased scalability, it also created trade-offs:

Any message produced had to be generic enough to remain accurate and relevant at a national level. Therefore, the message could not state that the recruitment event was likely to lead to a job, since this was not always the case. These trade-offs are a common part of policy and service design.

Once we had agreed to use the SMS system, the question was how to construct messages that met the solution requirements in fewer than 200 characters. A review of existing evidence had not revealed any clear best practices for encouraging this particular behavior. Therefore, we had to draw more on general principles from behavioral science, many of which we set out in the first three chapters. The process of moving from general principles to concrete interventions requires a book-length treatment itself; as we noted, the precise way in which a message is formulated or a choice is presented can have important effects on behavior. We can summarize two main aspects of the process here.

The first is to review existing evidence to anticipate how potential interventions will be received. You may want to revisit the findings from steps 4 and 5 that illuminate people's capability and motivation, and the context in which the behavior(s) are occurring (or not). You may wish to directly experience the context or service yourself again, with the potential interventions in mind. Your aim is to make a focused attempt to simulate the likely reactions of people experiencing the intervention. The difficulty here is that we often suffer from an "illusion of similarity" that produces inaccurate assumptions about what people think or know, as well as inaccurate predictions about how people will react to something.[4] In particular, the person creating an intervention may overestimate the extent to which others share their views or—because the creator is so deeply involved—the extent to which people will understand or engage with their work.[5]

Given these challenges, a second approach is valuable: presenting potential interventions to participants directly as part of the creation process. One way of doing this is to pre-test the intervention in low-cost ways. Assessing how the intervention affects a small number of participants in real-world settings can be valuable, if the intervention is low-risk and can be implemented cheaply. If not, an alternative is to create a close equivalent of the intervention and run a test with an online sample of participants.

The key priority here is to use the findings in the right way. Obtaining people's opinions about an intervention is useful for understanding how they will feel if it is implemented. But, while valuable, these findings are not always a good guide to how they will behave. For that reason, standard focus groups are generally less useful. If you are trying to understand behavior, however, then focus on the nearest equivalent to the real-world behavior and simulate the decision-making context as closely as possible.

Another option is to work with potential participants to develop simple prototypes of interventions. These prototypes can then be refined further or used to reveal new approaches. The advantage of prototyping is that it provides a much deeper engagement with participants' worldview, which may present new perspectives that were not accessible to the project team.

Whatever method is used, when creating a solution there is often a creative leap where evidence, theory, and context suddenly come together to bring a new possibility into view. While that may sound challenging to achieve, there are several helpful frameworks that provide more support for developing interventions. For example, the Behavioural Insights Team's EAST framework synthesizes much of the literature using four key principles—if you want someone to do something, then make the behavior easy, attractive, social, and timely.[6] Each of these categories includes several useful concepts and techniques that expand on what we have put here.

This process produced four messages for testing with Bedford Jobcentre. We now show each of these messages and provide a brief explanation of how we translated the relevant evidence into specific language. To give a sense of context, we present them as if a factory called SystemLink is hiring for security jobs. In each case, we have italicized any words that are different from the preceding messages.

A.   *Control.* The "control" message was the existing message used by the Jobcentre, which we retained because we could not simply assume that new messages would perform better.

> "8 new security jobs are now available at SystemLink. Come to Bedford Jobcentre on Monday 10 June at 11am and ask for Sarah to find out more."

B.   *Personalization.* A well-established body of research shows that use of a recipient's name is effective at attracting attention and making a communication seem more relevant. In this case, the system made it possible to insert the recipient's name into the message.

> "*Hi Elspeth*, 8 new security jobs are now available at SystemLink. Come to Bedford Jobcentre on Monday 10 June at 11am and ask for Sarah to find out more."

C.   *Endorsement.* Jobseekers are assigned a specific Bedford Jobcentre employee to advise them (a "job coach"). Our hypothesis was that mentioning the name of a specific individual that jobseekers had met could (a) signal that the opportunity was legitimate (b) connect the immediate opportunity to past and future conversations with the coach. We drew on a similar study that showed that showed loan repayments could be increased by including the loan officer's name—but only if the recipient had met that officer.[7] Again, it was technically feasible to obtain and insert the correct job coach name.

> "Hi Elspeth, 8 new security jobs are now available at SystemLink. Come to Bedford Jobcentre on Monday 10 June at 11am and ask for Sarah to find out more. *Michael*"

D. *Reciprocity and luck*. Many studies show that individuals often powerfully motivated to reciprocate actions—for example, to return a favor. In this case, we developed the phrase "I've booked you a place" to highlight that the JobCentre had invested some effort in supporting the event and inviting the recipient. We hypothesized that signaling this effort may trigger the desire to reciprocate by attending. We followed the phrase with a short "Good luck" message, which was informed by the concept of "locus of control." Some jobseekers are likely to have an "internal locus of control," which is the belief that someone's own actions can meaningfully influence what happens to them. Others will have an "external locus of control" and think that what happens to them is mostly determined by factors outside of their control. Jobseekers with an external locus of control conduct less job search activity.[8] At the same time, they may also be more likely to have a stronger belief in the concept of "luck."[9] Therefore, we anticipated that evoking luck may be effective for jobseekers in this camp, and increase attendance overall.

> "Hi Elspeth, 8 new security jobs are now available at SystemLink. Come to Bedford Jobcentre on Monday 10 June at 11am and ask for Sarah to find out more. *I've booked you a place. Good luck*, Michael"

You will notice that we created each message so that it builds on the next one, meaning that the final message contains all the preceding elements. This kind of additive design allows us to see the combined impact of the phrases, but it is less useful for isolating their specific effects. If we were more interested in those specific effects, we would structure the design of the experiment accordingly.

*Result of this step*: We designed four SMS invitation messages, informed by practical considerations and evidence from behavioral science.

**Step 8: Implement**

Steps 8 and 9 happen in parallel. In reality you cannot launch an intervention you plan to evaluate without also designing and implementing the evaluation itself.

In this case, implementation was quite straightforward. First, we needed to automatically generate text messages using the appropriate wording for each individual invited to a recruitment event. We built a basic spreadsheet to create the messages and upload them as a batch to the messaging system. This spreadsheet also used random number generation to assign jobseekers to one of the four message groups. To test whether the spreadsheet worked, we ran a prototyping process and fixed the small issues that emerged—for example, we shortened the original messages because they broke into two parts on older phones if recipients had long first names. We also checked whether attendance was being automatically and reliably recorded, and developed a procedure to handle people who had already been sent a message as part of the trial. We then supervised the use of the text generation tool for the first of the three recruitments involved in the trial period. For the later recruitments we simply checked the output messages for errors before they were uploaded to the texting system.

In other trials, implementation is a far more complex matter that requires active management and constant monitoring. One inconvenient truth of implementation is that the motivation of those charged with implementation will wane considerably as soon as the hassle factor of testing a new intervention exceeds that of running things the usual way. Small irritations loom large. For example, on another trial set in unemployment centers, BIT implemented a new process that required the use of a goal-setting booklet for each client. The booklets were of standard size but the desk drawers in which they would be stored were not. This created a huge hassle factor for the staff members who could no longer close their drawers and the inconvenience had to be fixed before it created irreversible damage. In most implementations there is a "desk drawer" moment, and the main takeaway is this: Do not ignore it. Whatever you or the project team can do to remove a burden associated with testing a new way of working will help ensure that the results of the test reflect the efficacy of the new intervention—and not the costs associated with managing the test.

*Result of this step*: Attendees were sent one of four SMS invitations, based on random assignment.

## Step 9: Assess the Effects

We have already alluded to randomized controlled trials (RCTs) in chapters 1 and 2. In this section we recap the basic premise of an RCT and give more detail on how to actually run one. While we use RCTs when possible, they are not always suitable as an evaluation method. Other analytical approaches are available; we do not cover them in detail here, to avoid turning this into a book on experimental methods.

Let's start with a quick recap of what RCTs are. RCTs are experiments that allow researchers to establish whether and how much an intervention has an effect on a particular outcome. More formally, they allow us to be very confident that one thing caused another (*causal inference*), which is attractive to those charged with protecting public investment or calculating returns on that investment. Causal inference sounds complicated but is a product of three simple features of the RCT.

First, well-constructed RCTs use *a large sample*. RCTs rely on splitting participants into groups. By including a large enough number of participants in each of these groups, we can be sure to gather enough data to iron out flukes, outliers, or other noise that might skew the results. A simple way to think about the value of more data is to imagine you are buying a product online. You have two different suppliers to choose from, both selling identical products. Supplier A charges $9.50, has an average rating of 3.5/5 stars, and has been reviewed by 1,000 customers. Supplier B charges $10.00, has an average rating of 4.8/5 stars, and has also been reviewed by 1,000 customers. Since you have 1,000 reviews apiece to go on, it is likely in this scenario that you can be pretty sure supplier B is better than supplier A and you can then make an informed decision about whether the difference in quality is worth $0.50 or not. However, if both suppliers had just ten ratings each you might be less confident about how meaningful their overall ratings are; one unfortunate experience could be enough to have hurt Supplier A's score unfairly. In

RCTs are experiments that allow researchers to establish whether and how much an intervention has an effect on a particular outcome.

other words, when there are fewer data and the difference is small, it is harder to be certain about any conclusions you may draw.

This isn't to say that small samples cannot ever be informative, just that you would need a much bigger difference in ratings (1/5 stars versus 5/5 stars, for example) to be confident in your inferences. It is the same way in RCTs: the larger the sample, the clearer the picture, and the smaller the effect that can be detected. A "power calculation" is usually used to compute the sample size needed to detect a specific difference between groups with a certain level of confidence. Power calculations use a mix of conventional assumptions, such as standard levels of tolerance for false positive (5 percent) and false negative (20 percent) findings, and trial-specific inputs. Along with these conventional assumptions, the simplest version of a power calculation also requires the researcher to specify two of the following: the sample size you have to work with; the expected effect size of your intervention; and the baseline level of the outcome of interest at present. Several websites can help you do this kind of simple power calculation for free. For more complex calculations, you may also need to know additional information, such as the variance within the sample.

The second key feature of the RCT is the use of a *control group*. As previously mentioned, we split the sample into groups: one for each solution being tested (often called *treatment groups*) and one "control" group that experiences the usual process. This control group provides a counterfactual. That is, the control group tells us—through the outcomes we observe for it—what would have happened if we had not changed anything (in this case, what would have happened if the preexisting recruitment event message had continued to go out with no modifications). In effect, this control group means that we are factoring in any other changes that might be affecting our outcome. For example, let's imagine we introduced our new messages for recruitment events in September, and then compared the attendance rates for those events against the ones held in August, when we were using the old message. If our new messages yielded higher attendance, we could not be sure whether that was due to the messages or some other factor. Perhaps the weather was better, perhaps there were fewer jobs available outside the events, or perhaps the event fell after a holiday when people felt more invigorated. Without a control group showing us the effect of the preexisting message on attendance, we might never be able to tell whether the higher attendance levels were because of our intervention. Of course, other factors inherent to the individuals could vary between the groups, which leads us onto the final design feature of RCTs: *random assignment*.

Random assignment means that people are randomly divided up into the control group or one of the treatment groups. Doing this randomly makes sure that the groups receiving each intervention have similar characteristics, which means that they are likely to behave similarly if treated the same. For example, in the case of event attendance, all the factors that determine whether someone shows up or not (e.g., whether they can afford the bus fare, the likelihood that they have other plans, their organizational skills, or their perception of whether the event is a valuable use of time) will be equally prevalent in each group. This means that if we introduce an intervention to one of the groups, we can say that any changes in that group's behavior are due to the intervention—rather than any other cause.

While it sounds straightforward, random assignment can be surprisingly tricky, and we advise running the process using a computer program wherever possible. Handily, even common software, such as Microsoft Excel, has an inbuilt function, =randbetween(), that enables assignment to a random group. Where it is not possible to use machine-led random assignment, proceed with caution. Even strategies that seem "random" can prove to have hidden bias within them. For example, in Britain house numbers typically result in odd numbers being on one side of the street and even numbers on the other. In many towns and cities, housing quality varies depending on the side of the street because of exposure to air pollution from factories during the industrial revolution; the direction of the wind means that houses with odd numbers may be systematically different from their even-numbered neighbors.

When planning an evaluation like this, it is important to document each of the steps, assumptions, and analytical choices that have been made. This will help avoid common pitfalls and also keep the person running the analysis honest when the data come in. By prespecifying what analysis will be performed, the risks associated with overinterpretation are minimized (more on this in the next chapter).

Figure 12 shows the evaluation plan for the trial in Bedford.

In this case, we randomized each individual jobseeker to one of the messages, but sometimes this is not the right strategy. For example, imagine that instead we were texting to workers within a supermarket information about a promotion opportunity: The outcome is still whether they attend a recruitment event, but it is held within their own workplace. Randomizing at the individual level is certainly viable but it is also risky. If everyone's phone beeps at the same time, and workers start to compare messages, then some may be demotivated because they have not been told "I've booked you a place." On the other hand, those who have received that message might infer they have a better chance. These perceptions change attendance; the demotivated go less often and their buoyed-up colleagues go more often. This spillover of treatments means that we cannot isolate the true effect of a certain message. Instead,

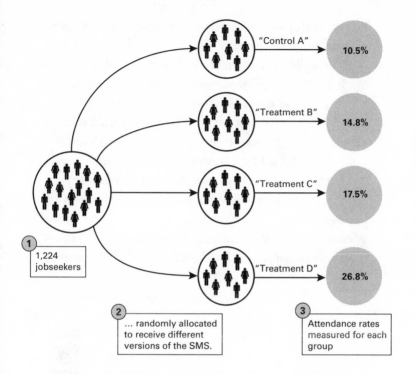

Figure 12

it would be more prudent, assuming this was a regional or national program, to randomize by store or shift-work team. That way everyone who is likely to compare their message to others is treated the same and the risk of spill-over is mitigated. This approach is known as *cluster randomization*. Of course, the point on sample size still stands:

We would still need to calculate how many stores or teams are needed to be sure of our conclusions (although the calculation is different when randomizing by clusters).

Finally, as RCTs allow us to estimate a range within which the true effect lies, we don't just learn whether something worked, but we are also gifted with a reliable estimate of its impact. The gray bars in figure 13 show the range of impact for each text message in Bedford.

Getting an estimate of the size of the impact is especially useful because policymakers with limited budgets (or business people with shareholders to reward) often need to choose which of several approaches give them the best return. For example, we are able to conclude not only that

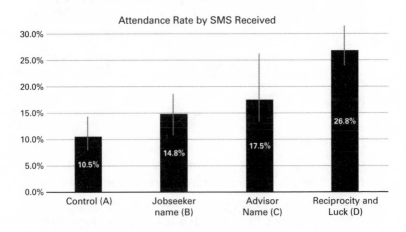

Figure 13

text D was better but also that it meant between 46 and 53 extra job seekers attended recruitment events during the trial period. When samples are large enough, we can also learn what worked for whom and attend to any differences or inequities that arise as a result (more on this in chapter 5). With unemployment, for example, we might be interested in whether these messages work differently for men and women, or whether recruitments for some skill sets are more likely to generate attendance than others.

At this point we reflected back on the goal set out in step 1: to increase attendance by 50 percent. Our intervention, although small, led to more than a 150 percent increase in attendance. There is still a good way to go, with 73 percent of people choosing not to attend, but this is a significant improvement both in the sense of statistics and policy.

*Result of this step*: We evaluated the intervention using a randomized controlled trial. The results indicated that the most effective message more than doubled attendance at recruitment events.

### Step 10: Take Action Based on the Result

Whether your intervention was effective, was ineffective, or even backfired, you will probably need to take further action to reap its full potential. Unfortunately, this step can be harder than many people expect. After all, adoption of a new way of doing things is a behavioral challenge of its own; just because something is proven to work does not mean it will be ushered in immediately as business as usual. Just because something was ineffective doesn't mean the plan to roll it out will be automatically wound back. Sometimes this may be for good reason. For example, an intervention that worked in one local context may not work somewhere else, and further testing is therefore required before scaling up nationally. Often, however, things will simply go with the flow of the default way of doing things.

In the case of our texting trial, we were able to replace the default message structure in the nationally held SMS system, meaning the solution was spread to unemployment centers across the country at the press of a button. This was, as stated in step 7, by design: we knew that expecting staff members in one unemployment center, let alone across the UK, to make a deliberate change to their standard practice was likely to mean our intervention never scaled. If we replace the default message with the new, more effective variant, then we are not requiring staff members to change their behavior.

Of course, improving attendance at a recruitment event is a relatively small change. As we mentioned in step 1, there are many other ways that we might be able to improve employment prospects for out-of-work individuals.

Thus, once success has been proven in one area, it is always worth returning to other behaviors or problems, if budgets permit. As mentioned previously, the approach set out in this chapter has also been used to fundamentally redesign the operating practices of unemployment centers.[10] From 2012 to 2013, BIT devised interventions in this category that led to unemployed people leaving benefits 1.5 days earlier than they would have otherwise. While this may sound small, this effect has large economic benefits when scaled: in this trial alone, more than 88,000 unemployed individuals were involved.

The solutions were devised and tested based on three months of research about how users experience unemployment centers, what the process underpinning the user journey entails, what the evidence can tell us about the experience of being unemployed, and how the process feels in practice. The new process involved shortening and simplifying paperwork; tailoring plans more to the jobseeker's life and routine; making meetings focus on future ambitions rather than past compliance; and improving jobseeker morale.

Scaling this intervention was very different from switching an SMS template, since it required significant buy-in from staff and managers. We spent a further six months helping to train trainers, producing videos to provide easy-to-access support, and working out how to supply the new materials to 700 unemployment centers across the country at scale. Now the process is embedded in all UK unemployment centers.

*Result of this step*: The message that performed best became the new default SMS template in the national texting system.

The behavioral insights approach has also been applied to employment policy in areas such as closing the gender pay gap, reducing hiring bias, and speeding up returns to work in the event of illness. Beyond this policy area, as the scope of this book shows, there are no limits to the issues that can be addressed by the approach. With such wide-reaching potential, we must, of course, be aware of the limitations, criticisms, and considerations that accompany behavioral insights. We turn to these topics in the next chapter.

# CRITICISMS, CONSIDERATIONS, AND LIMITATIONS

Thus far we have tried to offer a realistic sense of what the behavioral insights approach can and cannot accomplish. In this chapter we explore criticisms, considerations, and limitations of the field in more depth, while recognizing that we cannot assess them all in a short introduction.

We structure this chapter in three parts. First, we examine criticisms of what the behavioral insights approach has achieved in practice: is it only used in a limited way, do its effects endure over time, and how far does it produce unintended consequences? Second, we turn to the coherence, credibility, and generalizability of the evidence base. In particular, we explore concerns about the robustness of evidence in psychology and examine whether insights originally gleaned in the labs of Western universities can really tell us much about behavior outside the ivory tower and across cultures. Third, we explore the acceptability of behavioral insights, both through an ethical lens and from the perspective of the members of the public who may resent being "nudged" or experimented on. Our overarching point is this: The behavioral insights approach is not a panacea, and it is important to have a realistic sense of both its power and its problems.

## Does the Approach Deliver in Practice?

In this section we look at criticisms of the results that a behavioral insights approach has achieved. First, we consider whether the approach is being applied as ambitiously as it could be. We then examine unintended consequences, whether the effects we describe can endure over the long term, and whether these effects persist at scale.

### Limited Impact on High-Level Policy

As we have previously noted, behavioral insights can be deployed both in a tactical, targeted way and strategically to create wider change. However, many applications, in both the private and public sectors, have remained at the tactical level and involved tweaks to downstream features of a policy or strategy. This situation leads to the criticism that the approach does not tackle fundamental problems, but rather tinkers around the edges. Some critics go further, and claim that introducing nudges may actually reduce support for other, more powerful policy instruments. One study found that support for a carbon tax was lower when a nudge that defaulted homeowners into a renewable energy plan was also present.[1] However, in our experience decision makers do not think this way. They either understand that nudges complement (rather than replace) other approaches, or they see the use of behavioral insights as a way of strengthening standard policy options. The study itself shows that the crowding out effect is eliminated if people are told about the smaller relative effect of the nudge.

Nevertheless, we do think that it is important to understand the barriers to more strategic uses of behavioral insights. First, the prominence of nudging has led many people to think of it as the main or only way to apply behavioral science. Attention to nudges has often been at the expense of considering how behavioral science can bring broader changes. This perception is changing, but slowly. Second, specific interventions are easier to communicate quickly, and often provide a more straightforward story of impact: This change was made and directly resulted in this particular impact. In contrast, high-level policymaking tends to involve a fractured narrative of personalities, politics, and chance, all of which may remain confidential anyway. We ourselves focused on a simple, tactical example in the previous chapter, but this does produce a self-reinforcing narrative that other kinds of examples do not exist. The final reason is that the behavioral insights approach is an evidence-based, technocratic one—and it can be hard to graft this kind of approach into the messy, fluid initial stages of policymaking, where other factors often hold greater sway. A key point here is that increasing adoption of behavioral insights is itself a behavioral challenge, and one we will return to in our final chapter.

**Measurement Problems**

Behavior is complex. In some instances, a shift in one particular behavior mean that other behaviors move as well, in order to maintain consistency. But the opposite is also possible: Change in one area may lead us to compensate by moving in the opposite direction for another behavior.[2] For example, we have discussed how opt-out savings mechanisms for retirement are effective because they harness inertia. However, the power of inertia means that the default monthly savings level must be set with care. Set the level too low and workers gain a false sense of security about their retirement provisions without putting aside enough money. Set it too high and they find themselves having to borrow to cover expenses they might otherwise have been able to afford outright or with smaller loans.[3]

There are many examples of governments designing policies to target a particular behavior, without realizing that they may trigger other behaviors that actually create a bigger problem.[4] The behavioral insights approach may be particularly vulnerable here because of its emphasis on robust evaluation, and RCTs in particular. These methods are based on identifying specific, predefined outcome measures. But this precision risks creating rigid myopia. In the example just provided, looking only at opt-in rates for retirement savings would disguise the potential borrowing problems that may be mounting. In the final chapter, we discuss how behavioral insights should draw more on complex adaptive systems thinking to address this problem.

Another potential measurement problem is that behavioral insights may focus too much on the overall effect of an intervention, at the expense of understanding how its impact varies from group to group. While the overall result may be desirable, some groups may respond less well to the intervention. For example, receiving a home electricity report that compares a household's energy usage with its neighbors reduces Americans' electricity consumption by 2.1 percent overall.[5] But the size of the reduction varied between 3.6 percent for those who have left-of-center political views, live in an area with similar views, purchase renewable energy, and donate to environmental causes, and 1.1 percent for those in the opposite category (right-of-center views, no renewable energy, no donations).

It is especially important to check how vulnerable groups are reacting, in order to ensure that an intervention does not widen inequalities. On the face of it, though, there are reasons to think a behavioral insights approach may reduce inequalities. Traditional approaches have tried to influence behavior by providing information to change attitudes and beliefs—that is, through the Reflective System. However, more educated individuals are more likely to be the ones who seek out and use this information, which may widen inequalities.[6] In contrast, interventions that rely mostly on the Automatic System may reach the people who do not engage with the relevant information. For example, the biggest beneficiaries of introducing automatic pension enrollment in the UK were those on lower incomes, who had the lowest pension participation rates prior to the intervention's launch.[7] The flip side is that if the intention of an intervention is to exploit or cause harm, these groups may also be the ones that are hurt the most (see our later discussion of ethics).

## Longevity and habituation

Even when we are sure that an intervention has had an effect, we should be concerned about how long it lasts and whether the same results would hold if the participants were exposed to the intervention again. Critics have claimed that the effects of behavioral insights either do not last long after the intervention, or only work once, or both. Since the field of behavioral insights is a relatively new one, there is particular concern that the impact of its interventions will fade as they are repeated. This decay could happen for several reasons. One is that the intervention worked the first time because it was novel or promised some benefits of acting that didn't emerge. A long-term follow-up on the effect of providing energy reports to household consumers, for example, shows that the reports reduce consumption, but they have relatively less impact with each round.[8]

While this kind of decay can be measured within a single study, a broader concern has emerged as the behavioral insights approach has become more popular. Individuals may get exposed to the same kind of intervention by different actors, at different times, and in relation to different issues. For example, various studies have suggested that social norm messages may be effective, like saying that "9 out of 10 people pay their tax on time."[9] But what if this kind of message started appearing everywhere, in relation to use of public transport, choice of cosmetics, or exercise regimes? If the message is used too widely and inconsistently, people may start filtering it out.

The reality is that some effects do fade, but others do not—and we still do not fully understand why this happens. However, we can offer three overlapping ways in which behavioral insights can produce enduring change. The first is if a one-time choice has continuing, long-term effects (for example, opting for a long-term contraceptive method that does not require an active choice to use it each time). The second is to make changes to the choice architecture or environment that will repeatedly prompt the behavior on an ongoing basis (for example, redesigning a subway platform so that people's automatic reactions will always guide them a certain way). Third, external behavioral prompts may become internalized, so that the individual's motivation and attitudes become aligned with them. Internalization may occur from a single prompt or one that is repeated. For example, evidence shows that a one-time prompt that causes someone to vote can have lasting effects: With no further prompting, those same people are more likely to turn out in subsequent elections. Voting once, in other words, may be habit-forming;[10] making the first trip to the polls established enough internal motivation to overcome the barriers to future democratic participation. These mechanisms may overlap and be combined with others to create sustained change. For example, a study on financial incentives showed that while a one-time payment is not enough to drive sustained use of the gym, providing incentives to attend eight times led to a sustained effect, even after the financial incentives were removed.[11] In this case, the external prompts (payments) were in place long enough for the behavior to become internalized and sufficiently resilient to endure, even when the prompts were removed.

Of course, these three mechanisms do not guarantee a behavior will last. For example, a recent study by Katy Milkman and colleagues explored *temptation bundling*—requiring yourself to do something mundane or unpleasant in order to access something desirable. The intervention required students to visit the gym in order to listen to an audiobook of *The Hunger Games*. Creating this requirement was effective at promoting gym attendance in the short term. However, when the Thanksgiving break hit, the students returned to their baseline level of gym attendance: the intervention could not endure this disruption.[12] We think that this example may allow us to make a broader concluding point. The behavioral insights approach stresses the importance of contextual factors on behavior. Therefore, enduring effects are more likely if reinforcing prompts can be built into the future context or environment; relying on internalization alone may not be sufficient.

### Surviving Scale-Up

Once initial trials have confirmed desirable results, the interventions in question should ideally be scaled up and tested again to check whether the effects hold. While there are many examples of interventions that retain their effectiveness at scale, there is also evidence that some interventions prove to be less influential than they were in a smaller pilot. For example, a recent publication[13] reported on a campaign that tested ways to get 800,000 precollege high schoolers to take advantage of federal student financial aid in the United States. The size of the sample meant that several variations on the encouragement messages, some of which had proven to be effective in previous local studies, could be tested again. None of these messages proved to be effective in boosting either the receipt of financial aid or college enrollment.

The authors' reflections on why the effects may not have survived scale-up are helpful. They do not believe the difference shows that previous studies cannot be trusted. Rather, they hypothesize that some features of local campaigns may have contributed more to the original effects than previously understood. For example, students may feel more connection with a local organization sending messages or may perceive such messages to be more personal than when they are part of a national campaign. The result could also be due to the fact that this cohort of students are simply better informed about federal aid options. While the exact reasons are not known, the headline is clear: Things may work differently at scale, and it is important not to assume that results will be sustained without understanding how the features of the original intervention drove them.

Indeed, the behavioral insights approach offers two meta-lessons here. First, the details matter, so we should expect that small changes in context will alter the outcome. Second, scaling is itself a behavioral challenge. In the Jobcentre example, the mechanism for scaling was tightly controlled, so dependencies on new stakeholders adopting the intervention were limited. However, in most cases, scaling relies on those who were not involved in the original intervention deciding to act. When they do act, changes to the intervention can either prevent success or represent a necessary adaptation. In the final chapter, we discuss how qualitative methods can help identify which elements of an intervention should be preserved and which can be adapted.

## Are the Theory and Evidence Sufficiently Robust?

We have emphasized the pragmatic nature of behavioral insights. This section considers whether this pragmatism comes at a cost—specifically, whether the lack of a unified theoretical foundation stymies our ability to learn from the past and thus make progress and innovate. We also confront some hard truths relating to the evidence base. We examine the *replication crisis*, in which many seminal findings (notably from social psychology, but also more widely) have failed to replicate when tested again. In addition, we look at the implications of relying on studies that use homogeneous and nonrepresentative samples. Finally, we look at what we should do to protect the validity of future research and to ensure we are not building on shaky foundations when developing hypotheses to test.

## Is the Theory Incomplete or Overly Simplistic?

Let's start with criticisms of the underlying assumptions and theory of the behavioral insights approach. Some of these criticisms are esoteric, concerned mostly with creating a unified theory and neat taxonomy, and are best kept confined to seminar rooms and academic offices. Some, however, have more direct implications for how we diagnose problems and devise solutions to tackle them.

The first criticism is that the behavioral insights approach is too focused on identifying biases and deviations from rational choice theory. In this view, the approach has an overly simplistic view of what constitutes "errors" and "irrationality" that ignores the value of heuristic thinking.[14] Others prefer to emphasize the adaptive nature of heuristic thinking and its suitability to a complex world; we are better served by smart mental shortcuts than by some "rational" calculus. As such, they advocate the development and teaching of heuristics to help us better deal with complexity, an approach labeled "boost" (as opposed to "nudge").[15] While these criticisms might deviate from the way dual-process theories are viewed by (say) Daniel Kahneman or Richard Thaler, they remain compatible with these theories as a whole and do not fundamentally alter the thrust of applied behavioral science. Since there are situations in which heuristics are helpful and others in which they can be harmful, these perspectives are not irreconcilable in practice; a more useful focus would be on integration.

A related criticism is that the behavioral insights approach is too individualistic, partly because of its roots in microeconomics. In this view, the behavioral insights perspective adopts an overly cognitive view of people as individual decision-making agents, rather than as social humans who are embedded in established practices and networks. This means it has a "thin conception of the social" and little to say about culture or society.[16] What about the emphasis on how context and environment affect behavior? Critics respond that this is an overly psychologized view of "the environment," which only deals with "immediate, physical and technical aspects" and ignores the structural factors caused by institutional, economic, and political forces.[17] We think these critiques neglect the influence of social psychology on behavioral insights, but they have some force overall—we return to the issue in our final chapter.

Even if we do not question the dual-process paradigm, there is a potentially limiting shortcoming. Dual-process theories provide a catch-all, high-level explanation for individual "biases." However, they do not explain when and for whom these biases occur. For each bias there may be some evidence to answer these questions, but the picture remains incomplete without an account of how they interact with one another. We need more integration than just a list of stand-alone concepts under the umbrella of dual-process theories. This lack of a lower-level framework makes it difficult to determine whether a result is surprising or in line with expectations. As such, priorities for replication or further exploration may emerge haphazardly from the cherry-picked intuitions of individual researchers.[18] This leaves us unable to calibrate expectations and to build consistently on prior studies to shape the direction of future research over time.

Ultimately, though, the theory we have is enough to drive progress and development. Applying behavioral insights is about understanding the context in which a behavior is currently occurring (or not), so a unified conception of human behavior is neither necessary nor sufficient to develop effective solutions. Indeed, the results speak for themselves; we demonstrably have enough knowledge for successful applications.

Or do we?

### Bad Science: The Replication Crisis

In 2005, John Ioannidis published a startling paper. Entitled "Why Most Published Research Findings Are False," the piece introduced data showing that "for most study designs and settings, it is more likely for a research claim to be false than true." This counterintuitive conclusion is made possible by four common features of scientific publication:

1. Incentives and the "file-drawer effect." Journals prefer to publish exciting results, which typically means

studies that propose a novel hypothesis and provide evidence to support it. Failing to prove a new theory (in technical terms "failing to disprove the null hypothesis") gains little attention. Academics' careers are propelled by publications, so they are incentivized to invest most effort into studies that grab the attention of editors. The other manuscripts get left in the figurative "file drawer."

2. The standard assumptions of hypothesis testing. Conventional statistical practices accommodate a 5 percent chance of a false positive. Given the publication bias toward positive findings, this means that false positives are likely to be overrepresented in peer-reviewed journal articles. If twenty researchers all work on a similar experiment, chance alone means that one of their labs will produce a positive result that is fit for publication. That one result gets published and the other nineteen go back in the file drawer. Since people tend to research topics adjacent to other published literature, it is possible that many scientists are pursuing baseless theories.

3. Bad research practices. Small samples, too many outcome measures, and a host of other practices can produce effects that do not really exist. Small samples are problematic as they can result in chance findings being mistaken for real effects. Measuring multiple outcomes or too many variations of an outcome can also lead to

false positives because of the statistical assumptions already described: if twenty outcomes were measured on a given experiment, we should expect one to show a positive result purely by chance. Most research does not measure twenty outcomes, but even measuring five increases the chance of a false positive from 5 percent to 25 percent. Historically, small-sample research and research that cherry-picks the outcomes to report based on results have found it easier than one might imagine to find a home in prestigious journals.

4. While these research practices are fairly common, revelations over the last decade have also shown a rarer and much more egregious form of malpractice: Some researchers have been caught faking their data entirely. We will not discuss this further here since it is a rare occurrence, but it is a serious, if infrequent, contributing factor.

Ioannidis and other critics triggered a movement (albeit one that took another five years to really gain momentum) to interrogate prior research findings across a range of fields, including psychology. One such endeavor was The Reproducibility Project. In a triumph of academic collaboration, 270 researchers, led by Brian Nosek at the Center for Open Science, attempted to repeat and reproduce the results of 100 psychology studies published in 2008.

Of the original 100 studies, 97 had reported positive significant effects. Since experiments are conventionally designed to tolerate a 20 percent risk of a false negative and a 5 percent risk of a false positive, we should expect around five of the 97 to fail to reproduce due to false positives in the original and around 19 to fail due to a false negative in the replication result. In other words, if around 75 percent of the original experiments produced the same result when repeated, then there would be no need to cast doubt on the validity of research in the field.

This is not what happened. In fact, when The Reproducibility Project reported in 2015, it had only been able to replicate the positive results for 36 percent of the studies, and even then, the effects were often smaller than originally reported. A generous interpretation would point out that some results may have turned out differently because true replication is impossible: we cannot exactly reconstruct the conditions of the first test, the context in which it occurred, or its participants. However, it is likely that this accounts for only a small number, if any, of the studies, since the inclusion criteria for replication considered imitability, and the protocols explaining how the replication was done are convincingly detailed.

These studies are also not alone in their failure to replicate. Other findings in other academic disciplines have also proven elusive on second, third, and fourth testing. They include some seminal studies that have diverted massive amounts of research time and money. Collectively, these challenges have come to be known as the "replication crisis": a moment in the development of social science research that has forced serious critical reflection. But before we discuss what is happening to correct for the bias inherent in publication and how we can navigate this reckoning as practitioners of the behavioral insights approach, we must also acknowledge another threat to the validity of psychological research: its generalizability.

### WEIRD Science: The Problem of Generalizability

So far, we have explored the concept of *internal validity*: the extent to which the methods used in any given experiment can reliably tell us about causality. We have not, however, discussed *external validity*: the extent to which the results hold beyond the original sample. Here, much of the foundational behavioral science research suffers from a significant limitation: most of the canonical experiments were conducted with populations that are disproportionately Western, Educated, Industrialized, Rich, and Democratic—a group dubbed WEIRD for short.

Using WEIRD people as research subjects is problematic because their life experiences put them "among the least representative populations one could find for generalizing about humans."[19] WEIRD populations behave differently on dimensions ranging from visual perception to moral reasoning to risk appetite and present bias.[20] For example, a set of studies across fifteen small-scale societies[21] sought to test the extent to which prosocial behavior was exhibited by players in a series of economic games. Like their WEIRD counterparts, all societies demonstrated some degree of prosocial behavior, going against the predictions of rational choice theory. However, they varied considerably in the extent to which the prosocial behavior occurred. The variation does not appear to be explained by individual differences. Rather, individuals act in line with the norms of their societies, with factors such as economic organization and the structure of social interactions informing their behavior in the game. This finding adds weight to the argument that the contexts we live in fundamentally influence our decisions, meaning that even if a particular bias is universal, it will not always be possible to transplant an insight or intervention successfully from one setting into another.

The WEIRD shortcoming also presents some more fundamental concerns, notably in terms of what is actually being measured. Take, for example, the "marshmallow test," which is one of the most famous experiments in psychology.[22] Children are given the choice of one marshmallow now or, if they can wait fifteen minutes in the presence of the first marshmallow without eating it, two marshmallows. The experiment was long thought to measure self-control, a trait that is proven to be associated with a range of good outcomes.[23] This observed ability was then used to explain differences in life outcomes of participating children decades later.

However, a child who is used to receiving treats, and knows from experience that adults can be trusted to be true to their word, might perceive such a choice very differently from a child who has never known the luxury of a marshmallow and has low levels of trust because he or she has been let down before. For the second child, the promise of a second marshmallow is empty; to delay eating the first one is to risk losing out altogether. If this is the case, then the study may not have been measuring self-control at all. In the first study, the sample was small and the cohort unusual. All 90 children involved were enrolled in the Stanford campus preschool; they were likely to be from affluent families whose parents were highly invested in education. When researchers revived the marshmallow test, this time with 900 young children who better represented the US population, the results were quite different.[24] Once other factors relating to the children's backgrounds were taken into account, the link between holding out for a second marshmallow and improved outcomes in later life disappeared.[25]

Personality research is also affected by this issue of representation and measurement. In WEIRD-dominated research, the Big Five personality traits—openness, conscientiousness, extraversion, agreeableness, and neuroticism—are shown to be predictive of a range of outcomes, from job performance to mortality. However, a recent study including more than 94,000 respondents from low- and middle-income countries showed that commonly used personality questions failed to measure the intended trait and were not valid in these populations.[26] This destabilizing finding means that we must question the starting assumptions that led us to think we had identified immutable tenets of personality. These assumptions may have crept in as WEIRDness also pervades research labs. Increased diversity of thought and experience in the field might have prevented an overly narrow view of fundamental personality constructs.

These findings do not mean that the rich body of personality research or the original marshmallow test is not useful. Rather, it means we must be careful to question the extent to which the insights we gain from researching narrow samples are generalizable.

**What Should We Do in the Face of This Crisis of Evidence?**
Shaky foundations make it difficult to build strong interventions. Alongside correcting our understanding of past work, we also need to make changes that assure the validity of future research. Many academic publications have tried to change the fundamental incentives for those seeking to publish. Specifically, this means opening the "file drawer" by welcoming studies that fail to disprove the null hypothesis or that explicitly attempt to replicate an earlier

study. This change in emphasis tries to shift the emphasis from novelty to quality, making it less likely that bad research practices will perpetuate over time.

An important part of this drive toward better quality is to value or require "preregistration." Preregistration is where the plan for a piece of research is published in advance of the results being analyzed. Research can therefore be judged on its merits—in terms of both underpinning theory and evaluation strategy—before the results are known. Researchers therefore have less ability or need to come up with something headline-grabbing when the data come in. Some journals are going even further, and are peer-reviewing hypotheses and methods before any data are collected; if the foundations are solid, the paper will be accepted, whatever its conclusions. Assessing studies on these foundations leads to tighter scrutiny, higher research quality, and more reliable results.

Beyond academia, preregistration is good practice for any research, and it does not need to be an onerous process. Indeed, the activities involved—clearly stating what will be tested, how, and why—will help clarify thinking and improve quality, as well as holding those doing the analysis to account. Similarly, when assessing the merit of work that has already been published, publication alone should not be taken as an indication of validity. As consumers of research we need to be critical, looking beyond the basic question of whether a difference in outcomes was shown to be statistically significant and asking the right follow-up questions to qualify whether the result is credible and meaningful. These are the same questions a reviewer should ask: Is the sample large enough? Are the groups comparable? Is the size of the effect consistent with what we see in similar research? Does the outcome reported include all data? If not, why not? Does the outcome really measure what it claims to? Does an outcome of this size mean those who experience it benefit in a meaningful way?

We are aware, though, that people will only ask these questions if they have the capability and incentives to do so. The problem is that, as a developing field, the behavioral insights approach may not be creating these conditions yet, and still rewards only a superficial engagement with the relevant research. We return to this issue in the final chapter.

## Is the Behavioral Insights Approach Ethical? Is It Acceptable?

We deal with this—the closing section of this chapter— in two parts. First, we consider the ethics of deploying interventions designed to alter behavior. Then we examine whether the public considers such interventions to be acceptable. We deliberately do not include a discussion on the ethics of the experimental method; that issue goes well beyond the field of behavioral insights (which does not always use experiments) and has been rehearsed many times before.[27]

## Is It Ethical to Use Behavioral Insights?

Behavioral insights can be used in ways that are manipulative or against the best interests of both an individual and society in general. This is not an abstract risk. For example, "dark patterns" are widely used to coerce or deceive customers or users into making decisions that are against their best interests or personal preferences. A recent study of around 11,000 websites found that 11 percent of the sites routinely deployed "dark patterns," and that these sites were typically ranked more highly by search engines.[28] For example, companies often use the concept of friction to their advantage, making it very easy to sign up for their services and very difficult to unsubscribe. This specific tactic of introducing friction to discourage beneficial behaviors has recently been labeled "sludge," the evil twin of nudge. Criticisms of this kind are leveled at the public sector as well. Government may also introduce sludge, for example: there is increasing research into how governments may discourage certain groups from accessing public services by introducing administrative burdens that particularly hamper those with few resources.[29]

Behavioral insights can be manipulative. For example, "dark patterns" are widely used to coerce customers into making decisions that are against their best interests.

Having given some examples of ethically problematic uses, let's unpack the central sources of concern. There have been many ethical critiques of behavioral insights, but we think they can be boiled down to two main charges: one, that the approach is paternalistic; and the other, that it is manipulative. When we cover both of these points in the paragraphs that follow, our goal is not to find a way to rebut them; instead, we conclude by offering a basic framework to guide the responsible application of behavioral insights.

Concerning paternalism, we first need to identify what new problems the use of behavioral insights introduces. There is a danger that general concerns about paternalism are presented as specific criticisms of behavioral insights. On this score, the main charge is that the presentation of human decision making as "irrational" or "biased" justifies corrective action by government or others. For example, behavioral economics explores the idea of "internalities," which is where there is a conflict between someone's present-day self (desiring cake) and their future self (desiring to be healthy). This kind of theory and evidence provides a technical rationale for intervention to help the future self, who often loses out otherwise. In the process, the agent intervening will be deciding what behaviors are desirable and stacking the deck to make it more likely we will perform them.

The concern is that this view breeds an elitist professional approach that has a degraded view of citizens as being unable to shape their behavior independently. The insights from behavioral science lead choice architects to become overconfident in their assumptions about what people "really" want, and why they are acting in certain ways.[30] This is a problem because our preferences are not always clear, formed, fixed, and knowable, even by ourselves.[31]

Some critics go further, and claim that "behavioural economics itself undermines the case for paternalism" because policymakers are subject to the same biases they find in others, even if they don't realize it.[32] More and more studies are showing how decision makers are subject to confirmation bias, framing effects, group polarization, and the false consensus effect, among others.[33] Since they will also make errors, the argument runs, their interventions are unjustifiable. In other words, behavioral science reveals a fatal flaw at the heart of any paternalistic action.

The first thing to note is that the paternalism critique is aimed at those policies that try to increase benefits or reduce harms for oneself (e.g., saving more, eating healthily). It is less relevant to the wide range of government actions aimed at behaviors that affect others (e.g., reducing crime). Liberal democracies have long found the first kind of intervention to be more controversial.[34] The second point is that, as we discussed in chapter 1, applying a behavioral lens may not point toward trying to change someone's behavior at all. Instead, it may encourage reassessment of

Policymakers are subject to the same biases they find in others, even if they don't realize it.

existing government action, prevent a misguided policy from being introduced, or shape policies around existing behaviors instead (more on this in the final chapter). Even when influencing behavior is the goal, in practice the behavioral insights approach has often followed *Nudge*'s emphasis on libertarian paternalism as a freedom-preserving alternative to the harder paternalism of bans, restrictions, or fines.[35]

More generally, we think these criticisms concern choices about how to use behavioral insights, rather than striking at the heart of the approach itself. The idea of "irrationality" is neither central to behavioral insights nor particularly helpful. We propose that behavioral insights should be applied in a "humble" way that sets goals sensitively, based on trying to understand the reasonableness of individuals' actions, rather than holding a narrow, inflexible view of what is "rational" in a particular situation.[36] The latter would simply be bad policymaking.

Of course, to encourage this desired approach we would need to improve the way that policy or strategy is itself made, which brings us back to another of the criticisms already described: Governments and companies are themselves subject to cognitive biases. But we argue that this means that the case for using behavioral insights is stronger, rather than weaker. The behavioral insights approach is now being used to identify the biases introduced by institutions and processes—and to offer new ways of

The idea of "irrationality" is neither central to behavioral insights nor particularly helpful.

mitigating issues like overconfidence.[37] Nudging decision makers will address the problems of paternalism better than just ignoring behavioral science.

One final point is that many advocates of nudging make the argument that "there is no neutral design"—that some influence will always take place, even unintentionally, so it may as well push people in a beneficial direction. However, this argument has a clear flaw. In any judgment of human action, intentions matter—people feel this intuitively, and the criminal justice system sees it as a founding principle. The role of choice architect is accompanied by a level of responsibility. Those who have taken steps to shape someone's choices must be able to answer the question of what goals they are trying to pursue, and why—which loops back to the paternalism question.

The second concern is that the use of behavioral insights is manipulative. The critique here is not about straightforward deception or false content; we are assuming that these play no part. Instead, the idea is that if behavioral insights interventions involve nonconscious modes of decision making, then the recipients may not be aware of whether and how they are being influenced. They therefore are not able to easily resist the influence or debate and contest the intervention, either as citizens or as consumers. Moreover, many of the interventions are constructed precisely to be delivered in a seamless, unobtrusive way. In other words, it may be that "these techniques work best in the dark."[38]

Even where the outcome aligns with our preferences, if it is obtained through stealth, the intervention treats people as a means to an end, rather than as ends in themselves. Individual decision makers are denied dignity and agency to determine their own course and develop their own preferences. This can mean that the use of behavioral insights is disempowering and infantilizing, since people are denied the opportunity to reflect, learn, and update future behaviors.

One immediate response is that such interventions may not be manipulative at all. Some interventions are designed precisely to activate a more reflective mode of thinking to enable a higher quality decision. Indeed, this is the premise of the "boost" approach we referred to earlier. However, this kind of approach faces the obvious issue that we find it very difficult to apprehend our non-conscious behavior! In particular, we have a "bias blind spot": we tend to think that others are biased, but not ourselves.[39] And simply highlighting the existence of biases and urging people to be less biased can backfire and create more bias.[40] For example, in one study, people who were primed to feel objective were *more* likely to discriminate on the basis of gender when making a hiring decision.[41] Careful design is needed so the desire to avoid an unethical process does not end up creating an unethical outcome.

Another option is to rely on the "publicity principle": would the government or business be willing or able to defend the intervention if its mechanics were made public? If not, they should not proceed, since doing otherwise would mean a lack of respect for those they serve. The problem is that this seems like a weak requirement. Building on our point about the biases of policymakers, there would always be scope to practice "motivated reasoning" and rationalize why people would support a policy that you want to implement.

A stronger rule would be that all interventions have to be made public, either at the time of delivery or later. Many organizations have promoted this principle. As we discuss later, the public may support interventions that use automatic decision processes to produce desirable outcomes. Disclosure also may not reduce an intervention's effectiveness. People can be told how their choices are being structured, and why, without behaving differently as a result, although we need more research here.[42] The difficulty with these points is: What exactly does it mean to make an intervention public? How could this be done practically? More generally, how can we separate out what elements of government action could be considered "manipulative" or not? We think some criteria are needed to help us assess cases.

To meet this need, we offer a very simple framework for assessing the ethical issues surrounding behavioral insights. There are four factors, two of which relate to manipulation (i.e., how an intervention works):

*Control*: How easy is it for the relevant actor to resist the intervention, considering the context and their capabilities?

*Transparency*: How reasonable is it to expect that the target of an intervention will perceive its intention, at the moment of decision or later?

The other two relate to paternalism (i.e., what behavior is being influenced):

*Extent of consequences*: What are the likely harms and benefits of adopting or not adopting the behavior, and where do they fall?

*Strength of preferences*: How strong and settled are the preferences of the people being influenced? What is the strength of evidence informing this judgment?

Figure 14 shows that the two factors in each group inform each other: The level of transparency influences how much control people have, while the consequences of the behavior need to be weighed against the strength of intentions involved. Considering the four factors should offer a

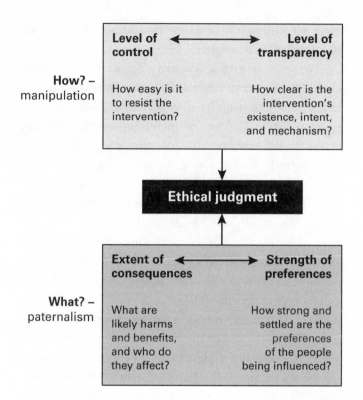

Figure 14

more structured way of assessing ethical issues with applying behavioral insights.

We want to give a few more details on this framework. One aspect of control deals with latitude inherent in the basic choices offered to someone. These are often presented as a "ladder" of increasing restrictions that starts at the bottom with just providing information, moving up to enabling or guiding choices, providing incentives, then disincentives, restricting choice, coercion, and eliminating choice.[43] We offered a simplified version of this scale in chapter 1 with our discussion of information, incentives, and legislation. Importantly, the intensity of influence can vary even on the same rung of this ladder—and this is the other aspect of control. For example, providing information could range from posting nutritional data for products on a government website, to a policy that uses all the resources from behavioral insights to make sure that consumers cannot avoid knowing what's in their potential purchases.[44] The key aspect is how easy it is to resist the intervention. How far we are up the "ladder" obviously matters, but so does how easily someone can resist their automatic responses to the intervention. We need to make a realistic assessment of this second aspect, using the evidence from behavioral science, plus taking into account factors like context, history, stress, motivation, and cognitive pressure (where possible).

Obviously, a crucial factor for resisting influence is to be aware of it in the first place, which brings us to transparency. The main question here is how easy it is for someone to become aware that they are being influenced in a particular direction.[45] To be more precise, we can see three levels of transparency, which build on each other: Someone is aware of the existence of influence, the intent of the influence, and the mechanism(s) it uses. Figure 15 gives some examples.

It is important to note that these levels do not map directly onto the Reflective and Automatic systems. It's not the case that the more the Reflective System is involved, the more transparent things are.[46] For example, the system of traffic lights works substantially because of our automatic association of red with danger and caution; we may instinctively brake (or speed up) when the lights change. But this reliance on the Automatic System, plus the intention involved, is all completely transparent. We are aware of how traffic lights influence us. On the other hand, we may get influenced in nontransparent ways even when our Reflective System is mostly engaged, as the magazine subscription example in figure 15 shows.

We want to spend less time talking about consequences and intentions, because they relate to paternalism in general, rather than to behavioral insights specifically. Yet they are still important. The starting point for considering consequences is whether the harms or benefits from a

| What aspects are transparent | Example | Probable reaction of person affected |
|---|---|---|
| None | Positioning food in a cafeteria so that people are more likely to select healthy options because they are more prominent | Probably does not know that they have even been influenced |
| Existence of influence | Inserting a "decoy" unattractive option to make a magazine subscription offer seem more appealing in comparison | Realizes that "something is unusual or different," but its significance is unclear |
| Existence and intent of influence | Introducing messages into tax reminder letters that try to persuade by using the "omission bias" (people anticipate receiving more blame for an outcome if they act than if they do not act) | Perceives that they are being influenced in a particular direction, but does not know exactly how |
| Existence, intent, and mechanism of influence | Painted green footprints that lead people to a garbage bin; highlighting the cost of missed hospital visits in appointment reminders | Understands the goal of influence and how its effects are being achieved |

Figure 15

behavior fall on the person who acts, or other people. The former is paternalistic; the latter gives government more scope to act. But even for paternalism, the level of harm involved is important. For example, in 2012 the mayor of New York City proposed a ban on the sale of sugared drinks in portions larger than 16 fluid ounces. This policy attracted much controversy, and a strong theme in the objections was that people's liberty was being removed and their intentions disrespected.

Compare this policy to a 1998 law in the UK that banned the sale of paracetamol (acetaminophen) in packs larger than 32 tablets for pharmacies and 16 tablets for nonpharmacies. This change reversed the upward trend of suicides and poisonings, saving an estimated 765 lives over the following decade.[47] The impact on freedom of these policies is very similar: in both cases you can still obtain the product, if you make an additional purchase. But we suggest that most people would perceive them quite differently because of the level of direct and immediate harm involved. One prevents a possible indirect contribution to obesity; the other prevents an immediate and direct contribution to loss of life. Consequences matter.

So do intentions. Obviously, the ethics of suicide become more complicated as the strength and consistency of intent increase, as debates about assisted dying demonstrate. Our final point is that we need to find reliable ways of understanding intentions concerning a behavior.

After all, behavioral science shows that our stated intentions vary greatly according to how choices are presented. Or people may reverse their intentions when it comes to act. Indeed, we may be presented with an ethical dilemma, whereby we need to act to confirm the strength of people's intentions. In the case of the painkiller packaging, for a substantial number of people the intention to self-harm was not strong enough to overcome the relatively small amount of effort required to go to another store.[48]

Ethics need careful consideration. But the reality is that many uses of behavioral insights can be quite quotidian: for example, simplifying processes, reframing information, or changing the timing of an intervention.

### What Do Members of the Public Think, and What if They Don't Like Behavioral Insights?

Public opinion is a common and legitimate concern for those implementing, studying, and critiquing behavioral interventions. Indeed, backlash against policy choices can impose political costs and divert administrative resources. In the private sector, meanwhile, one act of perceived overreach can irrevocably damage market share. So how do we gauge public opinion and the kinds of interventions that are more or less likely to attract a negative response?

First, we can turn to existing evidence. Research by Cass Sunstein and Lucia Reisch shows widespread, though conditional, support for the types of behavioral interventions (they focus on nudges) that democratic societies have used or considered in the past decades.[49] In contrast, government-imposed mandates attract considerable objections. We want to draw out a couple of factors that affect levels of support. Interventions that rely on the Automatic System can be less well received than those that draw on the Reflective System. This is not an iron-clad rule; such designs can be considered acceptable if they clearly represent the best chance of being effective, as may be the case for overcoming self-control problems, for example.

Support also wanes when the motive for the intervention is unclear or when the likely outcome is a choice that goes against the best interests of the person being influenced. For example, defaulting someone into making a charitable donation—a good cause but not in that individual's personal financial interest—may cause reactance, while defaulting someone into saving for themselves may not.

Politics may play an important role here. Researchers have found evidence for a "partisan nudge bias," whereby people think that the use of a particular behavioral insight is more or less ethical, depending on whether they support or oppose the politician who introduced it or the purpose it is serving.[50] When people are asked whether they approve of the use in general of automatic enrollment defaults, right-wingers will find them ethical if the example use was to increase claims by the wealthy for tax breaks, left-wingers if the example use was to increase claims by the poor for income support, and so on. Perhaps the most interesting finding from this study is that people do not have strong or consistent stances on the ethics of nudges as tools per se—their views are driven by the ends that those tools serve. A final point: some argue that the public may become more accepting of behavioral insights as use of the approach spreads. This is the concept of "policy feedback," which claims that "policies can set political agendas and shape identities and interests . . . they can influence beliefs about what is possible, desirable, and normal."[51]

Nevertheless, if applying our simple ethics framework raises red flags, it may be prudent and helpful to go beyond existing research and ask members of the public directly for their views. Citizen forums, in which randomly selected members of the public are asked to provide their views on a topic, are valuable twice over: first to understand public opinion more deeply, and second to co-design interventions (more on this in the final chapter). Perhaps surprisingly, we have found from our own experience with citizen forums that public opinion often favors more paternalistic interventions than we might have expected. For example, in our work with the Australian state of Victoria's Citizens' Jury on obesity, the public was clearly in favor of exclusion zones where unhealthy food cannot be sold and increasing taxes and regulating portion sizes for sugary beverages. These are all interventions that have attracted significant heat when proposed or implemented by governments without public consultation. The Citizens' Jury helped separate out a representative view from the loudest voices that typically respond publicly to policy proposals.

In this chapter we have considered some difficult challenges: The evidence base may not be as robust as it previously seemed; the effects and longevity of applied behavioral insights are not uniformly impressive; and ethical questions are not easily answered. However, it is worth noting that some of the criticisms we have outlined are actually mutually exclusive: behavioral insights cannot be both ineffective and dangerously powerful, for example. We end with a reflection from a group of academics who, by their own admission, started out in opposition to the behavioral insights approach. But, they write, "As we become more aware of [its] diverse nature . . . we found ourselves increasingly advocating some of its insights to policy-makers."[52] They suggest that there has been a "caricatured critique" of the approach that "underestimates both its diversity of insights and its potential significance, while overestimating some of its moral implications." We are inclined to agree.

# THE FUTURE OF BEHAVIORAL INSIGHTS

Ten years after the term was coined, the behavioral insights field is at a pivotal point. Its first decade saw the approach attract significant resources, generate attention globally, and expand rapidly into a dynamic ecosystem. Robust evaluation means we know it has brought results. But a clear-eyed look around shows that governments mainly still rely on economists for their core policy decisions; every day, people experience services that are far from easy, attractive, social, or timely; and experimentation often feeds into marginal decisions only.[1]

After this period of rapid expansion, some reflection is needed. The approach has proven to be more than a fad, but the movement is still in flux; its legacy is unclear. To fulfill its potential and have enduring impact, those applying behavioral insights must do three main things over the coming years: consolidate, prioritize, and normalize.

The approach has proven to be more than a fad, but the movement is still in flux; its legacy is unclear.

Consolidating is about developing more consistency in the way behavioral insights are applied, confirming the most reliable evidence and theories through replication, and determining how findings vary across cultures and subgroups. Prioritizing is about identifying and pursuing the most valuable new directions for behavioral insights, in terms of both new techniques and new applications. Normalizing is about how to integrate the behavioral insights approach into standard practices for organizations, so it can endure even if attention fades—even if we eventually stop talking about "behavioral insights" as a distinct idea.

We explore these three actions throughout this chapter. In broad terms, we start by discussing more straightforward technical issues about how we can upgrade and optimize existing practices in the future. We then move on to more challenging questions about the tensions inherent in the behavioral insights approach, tough choices its practitioners will have to make, and what will be required to ensure it survives.

## Consolidate

The preceding chapters have shown that the behavioral insights approach has developed mainly through practical application, rather than following a clear blueprint. Moreover, the growth of these practical applications has been rapid: We have not always had the time to reflect on what is being learned. As a result, the label of "behavioral insights" has been attached to a great variety of activities.[2] Nudging is an obvious example. Some have argued that the definition of nudge set out by Thaler and Sunstein has gaps and inconsistencies, and there may be truth in that claim.[3] But Thaler and Sunstein are also clear in what nudging is not: taxation or bans, for instance. Yet the term "nudge" has become so popular that it does get applied to exactly these kinds of interventions.[4] In the same way, "behavioral insights" has been applied to many activities that have little relation to the evidence and principles we have set out in the earlier chapters—and some initiatives that actively contradict them.

To a certain extent, we should be relaxed about these developments. Some of them represent valuable adaptations to new challenges (and we propose further adaptations in the following). Since the behavioral insights approach is a pragmatic one, practitioners can leave academics to police the boundaries of concepts like nudging. But there are also pressing reasons to sharpen the way we talk about behavioral insights. The very factors that led to behavioral insights being promoted successfully—intriguing experiments and accessible summaries—also mean that it can be easy to gain a superficial knowledge of the topic, even if real expertise is lacking. The result can be free riders who apply the term "behavioral insights" indiscriminately (often to poor-quality work). Over time, these moves dilute the overall credibility of the approach and confuse those who want to understand or apply it.

One response is to set out a clearer, tighter definition of behavioral insights. Others can then refer to this definition and use it as a guide to shape practices or call out those who are abusing the term. A stronger set of practices can also form the basis for greater professionalization—and we are already seeing the birth of associations that are planning to create standards and certifications. Of course, we are not saying that every application can or should conform with an idealized approach. But we do think there is a pressing need to provide a coherent account of what that ideal is—which was one of our main motivations for writing this book. Over the longer term, we must move beyond lists of individual heuristics and biases, and focus instead on their relationships with one another and how they fit with the dual-process theories that provide the foundations for behavioral insights.

As well as solidifying the scope and approach of behavioral insights, we need a discerning look at the underpinning evidence. Which findings should we be using or discarding? The good news is that this work is already being taken forward in a few different ways. One approach is to combine the data from existing studies and work out which concepts or applications seem to have the biggest effect (known as a meta-analysis). As more behavioral insights studies are published, more of these syntheses are emerging. For example, a recent study of nudges in general found many studies of defaults that had a large effect, but fewer studies and weaker effects for precommitment strategies.[5] Another study looked just at nudges to change food consumption.[6] It found that nudges that focused on shaping the environment (e.g., placement of food) had larger effects than those that focused on shaping opinions (e.g., nutrition labeling).

The issue with relying on existing studies, as we noted in chapter 5, is that the reliability of some of these studies has been questioned. Several concepts that attracted much attention have since been found to have shaky foundations, including priming, ego depletion, and choice overload. Therefore, ongoing attempts at replicating results are helping us to understand which concepts should be avoided. People applying behavioral insights should both pay attention to these emerging findings and respond the right way. For behavioral insights to have credibility over the long term, we need to be ready to admit that some of our findings may have been one-time results. More than anyone else, behavioral scientists should know that unwelcome information is vulnerable to confirmation bias and cognitive dissonance. Our main commitment should be to "what works," since the overriding goal is to have an impact on issues in the real world, rather than to maintain theories for their own sake.

Of course, simply thinking in terms of "what works" is not enough. The behavioral insights approach now also has a pressing need to work out what works for whom, when, and in what contexts. One way of answering this question is to get more variety in our data. We already discussed the need to involve non-WEIRD study participants in chapter 5, and more studies are collecting data on cross-cultural variations in psychology.

The other approach is to look for the variety in the data we are already collecting. In chapter 5 we touched briefly on differential effects: when interventions work better for some groups than others. Looking at subgroups within the data we collect on trials can help. While running too many tests on subgroups can lead to spurious results, done properly this can create new, robust findings about how groups respond differently to behavioral insights interventions, allowing greater targeting and better results. As computing power and statistical packages have improved, new data science tools have also emerged that can help us do this even more effectively. Predictive analytics, for example, offers new ways of detecting patterns in large amounts of data, which can then generate new conclusions. These techniques were recently applied to the results from an intervention in Mexico that tried to increase savings rates by sending different SMS reminders. The analysis revealed that the reminder performing best overall actually made women under the age of 29 much less likely to contribute than using the other in-terventions. In contrast, individuals aged 29 to 41 years increased their savings after receiving the same message. Predictive analytics offers a powerful new way of detecting these patterns.[7]

As the name suggests, predictive analytics can also help make predictions: It can identify groups that are particularly likely to, say, default on a loan, so they can be offered preemptive help. In our own work, we found that applying these techniques to basic, publicly available information allowed us to reliably predict which medical providers were performing inadequately, such that 95 percent of inadequate providers could be identified by inspecting just 20 percent of providers. The vision is that predictive analytics can allow quicker, more sophisticated identification of groups who behave in distinct ways, while behavioral insights can deal with the "final mile": designing the most effective interventions to influence those behaviors.

Currently, though, we just do not have this level of precision in matching nudges to groups and situations. At least, this level of knowledge is not public—it may be possessed by private companies. Behavioral scientists can draw on the best available evidence, but this still means that there is an element of guesswork or professional intuition in selecting which concepts should be applied to which issues or groups. The problem is that the judgments of behavioral scientists are just as vulnerable to bias as anyone else's. Hindsight bias is likely to be a particular issue. This is where, after an event, people think that the outcome was much more predictable than it actually was before the event occurred ("I knew it all along!"). When behavioral scientists are running experiments, the danger is that unexpected results swiftly become obvious in retrospect, and people forget how uncertain or mistaken they were beforehand.

One effective way of combating this bias when applying behavioral insights is to force yourself and colleagues—the more, the better—to make a prediction (e.g., "I predict Intervention A will perform best"). Then force those who made the predictions to revisit them once the results are known—perhaps by scheduling a delayed email. Comparing predictions with results has several advantages: it helps you to place the results in context and appreciate how surprising—or not—they are; it provides feedback on how knowledge of the area is advancing (or not); and it helps ensure that our judgments of our abilities are well calibrated. We think prediction rounds should become a standard part of a behavioral insights approach.

Correcting for biases in selecting interventions can only mitigate the problem, not solve it. The question of what works for whom and when can only be answered by combining more data of better quality, new methods such as predictive analytics, continued testing of interventions, and improved delivery systems (since the risk of errors increases with more complex targeting). A final note of caution, though: apart from the question of can we target interventions at particular groups, should we do so? Many countries have laws that guarantee individuals equal treatment from the public and private sector, regardless of their characteristics. If we find, as in the Mexico savings study, that women under 29 respond differently from the general population, it may not be appropriate or acceptable to target them on this basis. What seems to be more acceptable is when we target people based on their previous behavior—for example, if someone has been repeatedly late with their taxes in the past. But the line of acceptability is blurry, particularly as companies are now using predictive analytics to increase consumption in ways that may not benefit consumers.[8]

## Prioritize

As well as securing reliable and nuanced knowledge about what behavioral insights can do, we need to determine the priorities for pushing the boundaries of the field. One need is to broaden its methods and perspectives, in order to give a fuller account of what drives behavior. Some historical context is required to understand why this need exists. When behavioral insights first came on the scene, much of the research on behavior provided to governments and businesses was based on the premise that people gave accurate accounts of what they did, why they did it, and what they would do in the future. A typical project might be to run a focus group, discuss with participants why they act a particular way, and then ask them how would react to new options (e.g., a revised message or process). The responses would be taken as the basis for policy or commercial recommendations.

As we have seen earlier, findings from behavioral science suggest that this kind of analysis is flawed. These findings led early proponents of behavioral insights to shape their new approach in reaction to this usual way of doing things. The impact of identity, society, and culture as drivers of behavior was displaced by a focus on dual process theories instead. There was less asking people about their motivations and reflections and more observation of their actions. And behavior was installed as the main outcome measure of value, rather than shifts in attitudes or beliefs.

These are generalizations, of course—but the behavioral insights perspective was defined in opposition to these common practices in order to show what was new. Now that it has succeeded, the approach needs to broaden out, loop back, and incorporate elements it previously neglected (as well as new ones). This is already happening: applied behavioral science teams are now much more multidisciplinary than their forerunners. In Canada, for example, the federal team sits within the Impact and

Innovation Unit, a group that also prioritizes approaches such as design and co-creation.

It is also increasingly common to pair quantitative approaches, such as randomized controlled trials, with qualitative approaches that can illuminate why something does or does not work.[9] Although a good behavioral insights project will be built on an evidence-based theory of change (see chapter 4), sometimes we cannot be sure that the results were produced for exactly the reasons we hypothesized. Conducting qualitative research means we can build a richer understanding: Was the intervention implemented correctly? Did some aspect cause participants unanticipated problems? Even if the outcome was achieved, were there hidden emotional or economic costs for participants?

Take, for example, a project the Behavioural Insights Team worked on with the International Rescue Committee. The goal was to reduce the use of violence against children by teachers in a refugee camp in western Tanzania. On the scoping trips we used a range of methods to identify the drivers of the issue, working with social scientists who had deep expertise in qualitative research, experts in postconflict and displacement trauma, and—of course—culture and language interpreters. As we moved into the solutions phase we worked with designers to develop interventions that worked in context and, since we knew that teachers would need peer-led support, we used network mapping approaches to identify the most influential individuals within the peer group. We also sought advice from experts in cognitive behavioral therapy, since a key part of the intervention was to help teachers identify triggers that led to habitual violence in their reactions. These collaborations produced a more powerful and nuanced intervention.

At one level, this broadening out can simply be seen as a case of behavioral insights adopting new techniques. But we think that a more fundamental change could happen. There is a criticism that the approach can be rather mechanistic in practice: experts apply a theory to a practical problem, a change is made, and prespecified outcomes of behavior are measured. While this is a powerful process, it can also be quite linear and static, with one active party nudging and a passive one being nudged. There can be limited opportunities for people to provide feedback on interventions to improve them. In the eyes of critics, this setup creates a "psychocracy" of control.[10] Therefore, we think a priority is for behavioral insights to incorporate new thinking on more reflexive, dynamic and nuanced forms of change. Two promising areas are human-centered design and network analysis.

In its most basic definition, design is about how elements are arranged to achieve a particular purpose. Design always deals with things that are tangible, experienced, and present, rather than with abstractions or theories. Objects or services can be designed to create certain feelings or thoughts, or to invite certain behaviors. In this sense, the use of behavioral insights has always incorporated aspects of design: it is concerned with practical problems (like "choice architecture") and is sensitive to how the wording of a letter or layout of a waiting room can have a big impact.

However, the behavioral insights approach to design has been quite top-down: principles of behavior have been used to embed certain ways of acting into the local environment or context. Designing from principles in this way can be successful (see the iMac or iPod), but it has also been criticized for not paying enough attention to users. However, there has been increasing interest in "human-centered design" (or the closely related concept of "design thinking"), which focuses more on trying to understand a user's needs, map their experiences, and actively prototype solutions with them. Behavioral insights projects could draw on human-centered design more in three main ways.

First, human-centered design focuses on exploring people's needs and goals, rather than starting from a target behavior (as in chapter 4). Of course, when dealing with policy there are instances where active steps must be taken to prevent people's needs being fulfilled (e.g., people's need to commit certain crimes). But we think the goal for behavioral insights is to pay more attention to people's needs, while also using its tools to understand the strategies people are using to try to fulfill these needs.

A very simple example concerns "desire lines." These are the informal paths, created by footfall erosion, that show the shortest or most desirable routes taken by people—which may not be the ones provided by an official design. Some designers have started to see these paths as an opportunity, rather than a nuisance. For example, universities such as the University of California, Berkeley, and Virginia Tech (Virginia Polytechnic Institute and State University) have waited to see which routes people were taking to cross grass areas, before paving the routes.

The same principle applies in more complex situations. For example, recently policymakers in the UK have become concerned about capacity problems in the country's hospital emergency departments. These problems are perceived to be caused by people visiting emergency facilities with only minor ailments. The system planners have created alternative options (like "urgent care centers") that deal with such ailments in a more efficient way. However, they are not very popular. In this situation, policymakers could use behavioral science to persuade or nudge people to use the "correct" facilities. But a more human-centered approach would look at the "desire lines," and see that attending emergency departments is completely reasonable. People are confused by the role of the urgent care centers, which are also not prominent and not always open (unlike the emergency department). Therefore, they are using a heuristic for navigating the system—"go to the emergency department"—which is working for them, and which means behavior will be difficult to change. This insight points toward instead adapting the service so people don't have to change their behavior—perhaps by co-locating the emergency and nonemergency care. In other words, there could be a greater recognition of people's agency and more attempts to design around existing behaviors, rather than attempting to change them.

Second, human-centered design places greater emphasis on people's own interpretations of their beliefs, feelings, and behaviors. The behavioral insights approach does emphasize the need for immersive techniques like in-depth observation, as well as trying to use services oneself. But it has tended to be more skeptical of self-reports, given the automatic nature of behavior and the prevalence of cognitive blind spots. (However, one of the most famous books on human-centered design admits that "people themselves are often unaware of their true needs, even unaware of the difficulties they are encountering."[11]) We think there is room to give more weight to how people view their own experience, and to broaden out from the focus on revealed behavior.

Finally, human-centered design encourages active participation from users (and staff members). We noted before that there are some applications of behavioral insights that work by disrupting the Automatic System, making people pause and engage their Reflective System. For example, the Becoming a Man program for crime reduction appears to work by "helping youth slow down and reflect whether their automatic thoughts and behaviors are well suited to the situation they are in, and whether the situation could be construed differently."[12] The program, based in Chicago, reduced arrest rates by 28–35 percent and increased graduation rates by 12–19 percent.

The obvious next priority is to combine these kinds of approaches with human-centered design to help people design or redesign their own environments. This relates to Thaler and Sunstein's vision that nudging can be used widely by "workplaces, corporate boards, universities, religious organizations, clubs, and even families."[13] But it also taps into the facet of behavioral science that claims individuals usually use heuristics effectively and can be empowered to use them better.[14]

Of course, there are many environments that individuals struggle to change on their own, indicating that a change in politics or policy is needed. As we discussed in the last chapter, there is a particular case for using the tools of deliberative democracy to discuss policies that draw on behavioral science. But this kind of engagement has wider potential benefits than just debating or approving certain policies—it is also important for a healthy democracy and civic agency.[15] And, despite what critics allege, the use of behavioral insights can actually help build that agency.

At the most basic level, behavioral insights can be used to nudge people to take part in civic activities in the first place. Although this nudge may be operating on the Automatic System, the goal is to ensure that someone takes part in an activity that engages their Reflective System. Then, behavioral insights can be used to design better deliberative mechanisms. Many of these activities take place in groups, but behavioral science shows that groups are vulnerable to issues like group polarization, availability cascades, and self-censorship.[16] We can't just assume that good reasoning prevails in deliberative settings—but evidence-based design makes it more likely.[17]

Finally, behavioral insights can spark wider engagement. Let's return to the example of food consumption from chapter 1. If people actively engage with the evidence that our eating is heavily influenced by features in our immediate environment, they may start requesting policies that address those forces. Indeed, there were signs that this happened in the deliberative forum on obesity in Victoria, mentioned in the preceding chapter, which produced fairly radical proposals. Behavioral insights could have an additional role here, by finding new ways to nudge governments or legislators themselves—and there is evidence that these attempts can actually produce results.[18]

This potential is not restricted to the public sector: People could also try to nudge companies. For example, the UK saw the creation of a Fair Tax Mark, which was awarded by a not-for-profit organization to businesses that did not practice any form of tax avoidance. The Fair Tax Mark is a classic nudge, in that it provides a prominent signal to consumers that can shape both consumer and business behavior, without mandating change. But this nudge was created through self-organization to achieve a particular policy goal.

Human-centered design can go a long way toward engaging behavioral insights with human agency more deeply, moving it further away from a mechanistic world-view, and opening up new frontiers. We think that network analysis holds similar promise. Network analysis concerns how behaviors spread through interactions. The behavioral insights approach has not neglected this question, owing to its roots in social psychology, but it needs to incorporate more of the latest evidence on the topic. While there are many varieties of network analysis, we think that a complex adaptive systems (CAS) approach could be particularly useful. In short, a CAS is a dynamic network of many agents who each act according to individual strategies or routines and have many connections with each other. They are constantly both acting and reacting to what others are doing, while also adapting to the environment they find themselves in. Because actors are so interrelated, changes are not linear or straightforward: Small changes can cascade into big consequences; equally, major efforts can produce little apparent change.[19]

An important point is that coherent behavior can emerge from these interactions—the system as a whole can produce something more than the sum of its parts. While we accept that this is true for things like markets, forests or cities, we are only beginning to understand just how pervasive network effects are. For example, a recent study showed how partisan policy divisions may actually be produced by chance, not prior conviction.[20] This US-focused experiment recruited participants who identified as either Democrats or Republicans. Participants were placed into one of ten online "worlds," in which they were asked whether they agreed or not with twenty statements. These twenty statements were about public issues, but had been constructed so that they did not tap into preexisting partisan fault lines. Rather than asking about abortion or gun rights, the questions asked whether participants agreed with statements like "the current lottery based juror system should be replaced with full-time licensed professional jurors" or "social media sites have a positive influence on people's daily lives."

The twist was that in eight of the worlds the participants were told whether mostly Democrats or Republicans were supporting the measure. The political alignment of others on the issues was made visible. But in two of the worlds, participants were not told about the views of others—they were just asked whether they agreed with the statements. The results were striking. When people were not aware of the views of others, there were hardly any differences between Democrats and Republicans in terms of support for the measures. When people could see how others were rating the statements, a strong partisan divide opened up—people aligned with their party.

But here's the fascinating part. The topics that fell into the "Democrat" or "Republican" camps varied greatly between the eight different worlds. Sometimes Republicans ended up supporting a new juror system, and sometimes they opposed it. Rather than views reflecting some preexisting ideological stance, partisan alignment seems to be created by "a tipping process that might just as easily have tipped the other way." The same system effects that lead certain songs or books to become unexpectedly popular[21] also drive some apparently fundamental and intractable problems in society.

Network analysis (and CAS in particular) can help the behavioral insights approach by making it less static, individualistic, and mechanistic. It offers new ways of understanding the impact of interventions that may not be captured by the linear process of RCTs. For example, an experiment in Austria showed that mailing different messages to 50,000 potential television license fee evaders increased their compliance.[22] This is a classic intervention along the lines of our example in chapter 4.

But the authors dug deeper and did follow-up analyses. Using location data, they mapped who lived near whom. They found that a household's compliance increased if its neighbors in the same network received a letter—even if the household did not receive one itself.[23] In other words, the behavioral effects of the intervention were spreading through social networks, as people told their neighbors about it. In fact, these effects were about as large as the impact of receiving the letter itself—5 to 7 percentage points increase in compliance.

The behavioral insights approach needs more of this kind of analysis. Many RCTs would not measure these kinds of spillovers and would focus only on the individuals who received an intervention. In fact, often the whole point of an RCT is to protect a control group against this kind of "contamination." Instead, we need to draw more on network analysis to understand how behaviors spread—and how this varies according to different types of behaviors—in order to maximize the impact of interventions. We need "nudge plus networks."[24]

There is a final, broader way that CAS can help. As we noted earlier, behavioral insights projects often take a fairly top-down and linear approach to designing and implementing solutions. However, in complex adaptive systems there may not be a straightforward link between causes and effects. As Herbert Simon observed in 1969, this means we need a different and less directive approach: "When we come to the design of systems as complex as cities, or buildings, or economies, we must give up the aim of creating systems that will optimize some hypothesized utility function." Instead, we need to understand how we can create the conditions so that individuals and organizations can interact in a way that means the desired behaviors emerge from the system indirectly.

We have made a start. There is increasing interest in behaviorally informed regulation that focuses more on reshaping the "rules of the game" for public good, rather than trying to target specific behaviors.[25] But the truth is that many behavioral scientists join policymakers in suffering from an "illusion of control."[26] This is where we overestimate how much direct impact a policy or intervention will have over events. We are particularly likely to do this if we are dealing with complex adaptive systems where change is not linear—so there is a pressing need to understand how behaviors emerge in those situations.

## Normalize

We have written about the need to consolidate the knowledge base for the behavioral insights approach, and the

We need to understand how we can create the conditions so that individuals and organizations can interact in a way that means the desired behaviors emerge from the system.

new methods that the approach should prioritize. We want to end by returning to the question at the start of the chapter: how can the behavioral insights approach fulfill its potential?

One obvious route is for decision makers to apply behavioral insights to a range of new problems. The development of driverless vehicles, for example, may not seem to have an obvious connection to human behavior. However, governments and developers around the world are coming to a different conclusion. When Singapore's Ministry of Transport set up its Committee on Autonomous Road Transport, for example, it invited our colleague Rory Gallagher to be a member.

Rory's role was to identify (and propose solutions to) challenges that might arise as a result of the pesky humans. For example, the illusion of control might lead drivers to think they have more sway over whether they get from A to B safely than they actually do, which could lead them to intervene in counterproductive ways. Similarly, one of the most famous examples of superiority bias—the tendency to think oneself better than average—is in self-assessment of driving skills.[27] If most people think they are better than average at driving, then will they be willing to relinquish control to a computer when the rubber, literally, hits the road? We think that the growth of behavioral insights means that decision makers are less likely to see these kinds of problems as purely technological ones.

But not all problems have the same importance—and the criticism we outlined in chapter 5 is that the behavioral insights approach has not had enough impact on the big issues in "upstream" strategic decision making, even though it could contribute much there. To generate that impact, we need to recognize that the solution here is not a technical one that improves the methods of behavioral insights. Instead, we need to see this as a political issue.

Research shows that, in reality, behavioral insights teams and experts are acting as "knowledge brokers" and entrepreneurs.[28] The successful ones recognize the often chaotic nature of turning ideas into practice (whether in the private or public sector), and look for windows of opportunity where they can prove their value. They are looking to develop networks, positions, and tactics that establish their authority and credibility among decision makers. Thus, the real need is to develop the skills of knowledge brokering in order to get the opportunities to influence "upstream" decision making.

The challenge is that this need creates tension between the three pillars of the behavioral insights approach that we outlined in chapter 1: the commitment to pragmatism gets pitched against the commitment to evidence and evaluation. Always inflexibly pushing for a randomized trial may result in behavioral experts being shut out of upstream decision making. So may failing to recognize that a comprehensive evidence review is not always possible, and that policymaking has to incorporate both evidence and political values. On the other hand, adapting behavioral insights principles too radically cuts against the need for coherence that we discussed earlier in this chapter.

Therefore, the way to build behavioral insights into upstream decision making is to create a productive balance between rigor and pragmatism. Pragmatism ensures the seat at the table, while rigor gives a better chance of successful outcomes. The longer term goal is that having such a seat at the table will start to improve the way policy and strategy are made in general. The truth is that there are many biases that affect policymaking itself, and we already have proposals that could mitigate them—the key is to get the opportunity to implement these.[29]

This brings us to our final point. Over the past ten years, there has been increasing interest in the idea of behavioral insights. However, at some point, this interest may start to ebb and attention may go elsewhere. Other ideas may come along, with their own compelling claims. People may stop deciding to "bring in" behavioral experts, as Rory was for autonomous vehicles. If this is true, then the immediate priority should be to integrate behavioral insights into the standard way that policy is made or organizations are run. That would mean that the practices are resilient to people no longer asking for "behavioral" solutions.

In fact, you could argue that this is the ultimate goal of the behavioral insights approach. The idea of a "behavioral"

The idea of a "behavioral" solution or approach should become meaningless, since the principles will have become absorbed into standard ways of working.

solution or approach should become meaningless, since the principles will have become absorbed into standard ways of working. Since, as we said in chapter 1, most policies or services concern behavior, then this is just about improving the way that central function is performed—it is not some kind of optional extra. Rather than talking about "behavioral public policy," we would just refer to public policy (or corporate strategy) done better. In a sense, stopping talking about behavioral insights may actually be a sign that its true promise has been fulfilled. Until then, there is more to do.

# GLOSSARY

**Availability heuristic**
The tendency to infer that things that spring to mind easily are more important or more likely to happen.

**Behavioral economics**
The study of how economic behavior is influenced by factors that are not fully represented in (or that conflict with) neoclassical economic thinking. Behavioral economics uses findings and methods from other disciplines, such as psychology, sociology, and anthropology.

**Behavioral insights**
An approach that applies evidence of the conscious and nonconscious drivers of human behavior to practical issues and evaluates the results, wherever possible.

**Behavioural Insights Team (a.k.a. the Nudge Unit)**
A team set up inside the UK government in 2010 with the remit to apply "a more realistic model of human behavior" to policies and services.

**Big Five**
A widely used taxonomy of personality traits, consisting of five dimensions: openness; conscientiousness; extraversion; agreeableness; and neuroticism.

**Bounded rationality**
An account of human decision making that proposes that people seek a good enough option ("satisfice") rather than the optimal option ("maximize") when making a choice.

**Choice architecture**
The way in which choices are structured and presented.

**COM-B**
A model that proposes three factors involved in producing a behavior: capability, opportunity, and motivation.

**Complex adaptive systems (CAS)**
A dynamic network of many agents, which each act according to individual strategies or routines and have many connections with each other. These agents adapt and self-organize, which means that changes are not linear or straightforward and the behavior of the whole cannot be predicted from its constituent parts.

**Compromise effect**
The tendency to "go with the middle option" when presented with a set of options.

**Confirmation bias**
The tendency to seek out, pay attention to, and remember information that confirms a preexisting belief.

**Control**
The group in a randomized experiment that receives no additional intervention beyond business as usual.

**Dark patterns**
The use of choice architecture to sway the decision maker toward an outcome that is not in the decision maker's best interests.

**Default**
The preselected option that will be taken if no action is taken to override it.

**Deliberative forums/citizen juries**
Involving the public to help inform policy principles and goals by gathering a representative view of what is desired and acceptable.

**Design thinking and human-centered design**
Deploying design principles to understand people's needs and shape processes, policies, products, and services to best meet those needs.

**Dual-process theories**
Theories that have the common underpinning principle that people have two main ways of thinking: one slow, reasoned, and deliberative, and the other fast, associative, and automatic. Daniel Kahneman characterizes these dual

modes of thought as System 1 (fast) and System 2 (slow); Richard Thaler and Cass Sunstein call them the Automatic and Reflective systems.

## EAST
A framework for organizing insights from behavioral science. Its core principle is that behavior is more likely to happen if it is easy, attractive, social, and timely.

## Ecological rationality
The idea that the rationality of a decision depends on the context in which it takes place, rather than being based on fixed principles. Heuristics may therefore be the best way of making decisions if they fit well with the environment.

## External validity
The extent to which the results from one study are generalizable beyond the test population.

## False negative
A result from a statistical test that indicates there is no significant difference between the treatment and intervention groups where, in reality, a difference exists.

## False positive
A result from a statistical test that indicates there is a significant difference between the treatment and intervention groups where, in reality, none exists.

## File drawer effect
The overrepresentation of interesting, novel, or surprising results in academic publications owing to factors that drive researchers to leave their unsurprising or null results in "the file drawer," rather than putting them forward for publication. Not only does this effect skew perceptions of how likely it is that the average research project will be novel, it also means false positive results are more likely to be published.

## Framing
The way in which information is presented, especially in terms of emphasis or order. For example, the following phrases are identical in meaning but vary in frame: nine out of ten people pay their tax on time; one out of ten people do not pay their tax on time.

**Heuristic**
A simplified rule, or rule of thumb, that can be used to help make a decision with complex informational inputs. Heuristics are practical, producing results that are sufficient but may not be optimal.

*Homo economicus*
A decision agent that makes decisions solely on the basis of what will maximize value for itself. *Homo economicus* makes consistent decisions over time, has infinite willpower, and considers all information when making a decision.

**Internal validity**
The extent to which the methods used in any given experiment can reliably allow the researcher to infer causality.

**Intervention**
A planned action taken to achieve a particular outcome.

**Loss aversion**
The tendency to seek to minimize losses, even when the cost of doing so is likely to outweigh the benefits.

**Mental accounting**
The tendency to place money in certain mental "accounts" linked to particular purposes, and to resist moving money between these accounts. This tendency goes against standard economic theory, which treats money as fungible (i.e., can be used for any purpose).

**Mere exposure effect**
The phenomenon whereby familiarity (repeated exposure) to an object or person leads to people liking that thing more.

*Nudge*
An influential 2008 book by Richard Thaler and Cass Sunstein that introduced the concept of "nudging."

**Nudging**
Designing choice architecture to make it more likely that a decision maker will choose one option over another. These designs incorporate evidence of the

nonconscious drivers of behavior, preserve the right to choose, and seek to advance the interests of the decision maker.

### Null hypothesis
The hypothesis that there is no difference in outcomes between the treatment(s) and control groups in an experiment. The null hypothesis is the starting assumption for an experiment, and is rejected if an appropriate statistical test shows a significant difference between the groups.

### Omission bias
The tendency to favor not acting over acting when faced with a decision that requires one or the other, partly because we anticipate that not acting will attract less blame. For example, we judge people less harshly if they fail to administer an antidote than if they poison someone.

### Overconfidence
The tendency for our subjective confidence in our abilities or judgments to be higher than our actual competencies.

### Peak-end effect
The tendency to judge the quality of an experience based on its peak and final moments, minimizing everything else about the experience as a result.

### Power calculation
A calculation that uses inputs on the key features of experiment to determine statistical power.

### Predictive analytics
Applying analytic techniques to large datasets to predict future behavior using information on what people did in the past.

### Randomized controlled trial/experiment/evaluation
An evaluation method that allows the experimenter to infer whether an intervention affected a measured outcome. It does this by creating a control group, randomly allocating participants to this group or a group that received an intervention, and comparing the outcomes for the groups. See chapter 4 for details.

### plication crisis
The failure of many seminal experiments in psychology and scientific fields to find the same results when rerun.

### Sludge
A specific form of "dark pattern" in which friction or hassle is introduced into a process to discourage the user from completing it.

### Social proof/social norms
The tendency to take our cues from others and behave in line with our perceptions of what is normal or usual.

### Statistical power
The probability that an experiment rejects the null hypothesis when a difference in outcomes of the treatment and control groups truly exists. Statistical power ranges from 0 to 1. As power increases, the chance of a false negative result decreases.

### Temptation bundling
Pairing a necessary but unappealing activity with one that is appealing in order to motivate completion of the unappealing activity.

### Treatment group
The group in a randomized experiment where members receive the intervention.

### Utility
A unit of measure that denotes the value of an activity, good, or service for the consumer or beneficiary.

### WEIRD population
A study population, overrepresented in academic literature, that is primarily from a culture that is Western, Educated, Industrialized, Rich, and Democratic.

# NOTES

**Chapter 1**

1. Alexander Chernev and David Gal, "Categorization Effects in Value Judgments: Averaging Bias in Evaluating Combinations of Vices and Virtues," *Journal of Marketing Research* 47, no. 4 (2010): 738–747.

2. Natalina Zlatevska, Chris Dubelaar, and Stephen S. Holden, "Sizing Up the Effect of Portion Size on Consumption: A Meta-Analytic Review," *Journal of Marketing* 78, no. 3 (2014): 140–154.

3. Gareth J. Hollands, Ian Shemilt, Theresa M. Marteau, Susan A. Jebb, Hannah B. Lewis, Yinghui Wei, Julian P. T. Higgins, and David Ogilvie, "Portion, Package or Tableware Size for Changing Selection and Consumption of Food, Alcohol and Tobacco," *Cochrane Database of Systematic Reviews* 9 (2015).

4. Barbara J. Rolls, Erin L. Morris, and Liane S. Roe, "Portion Size of Food Affects Energy Intake in Normal-Weight and Overweight Men and Women," *American Journal of Clinical Nutrition* 76, no. 6 (2002): 1207–1213.

5. Thomas L. Webb and Paschal Sheeran, "Does Changing Behavioral Intentions Engender Behavior Change? A Meta-Analysis of the Experimental Evidence," *Psychological Bulletin* 132, no. 2 (2006): 249.

6. Mark R. Leary and Robin M. Kowalski, "Impression Management: A Literature Review and Two-Component Model," *Psychological Bulletin* 107, no. 1 (1990): 34.

7. Department of Health, "Health Survey for England 2008" (London: HMSO, 2009).

8. Uzma Khan and Daniella M. Kupor, "Risk (Mis) Perception: When Greater Risk Reduces Risk Valuation," *Journal of Consumer Research* 43, no. 5 (2017): 769–786.

9. Loran F. Nordgren, Frenk Van Harreveld, and Joop Van Der Pligt, "The Restraint Bias: How the Illusion of Self-Restraint Promotes Impulsive Behavior," *Psychological Science* 20, no. 12 (2009): 1523–1528.

10. Marieke A. Adriaanse, Charlotte D. W. Vinkers, Denise T. D. De Ridder, Joop J. Hox, and John B. F. De Wit, "Do Implementation Intentions Help to Eat a Healthy Diet? A Systematic Review and Meta-Analysis of the Empirical Evidence," *Appetite* 56, no. 1 (2011): 183–193.

11. Barbara J. Rolls, Liane S. Roe, and Jennifer S. Meengs, "Reductions in Portion Size and Energy Density of Foods Are Additive and Lead to Sustained

Decreases in Energy Intake," *American Journal of Clinical Nutrition* 83, no. 1 (2006): 11–17.

12. L. K. Bandy, P. Scarborough, R. A. Harrington, M. Rayner, and S. A. Jebb, "Reductions in Sugar Sales from Soft Drinks in the UK from 2015 to 2018," *BMC Medicine* 18, no. 1 (2020): 20.

13. Public Health England, *Calorie Reduction: The Scope and Ambition for Action* (London: HMSO, 2018).

14. Susan E. Sinclair, Marcia Cooper, and Elizabeth D. Mansfield, "The Influence of Menu Labeling on Calories Selected or Consumed: A Systematic Review and Meta-Analysis," *Journal of the Academy of Nutrition and Dietetics* 114, no. 9 (2014): 1375–1388.

15. Richard H. Thaler and Cass R. Sunstein, *Nudge: Improving Decisions about Health, Wealth, and Happiness* (New Haven, CT: Yale University Press, 2008).

16. Itamar Simonson, "Choice Based on Reasons: The Case of Attraction and Compromise Effects," *Journal of Consumer Research 16,* no. 2 (1989): 158–174.

17. Kathryn M. Sharpe, Richard Staelin, and Joel Huber, "Using Extremeness Aversion to Fight Obesity: Policy Implications of Context Dependent Demand," *Journal of Consumer Research* 35, no. 3 (2008): 406–422.

18. Kelly Ann Schmidtke, Derrick G. Watson, Pendaran Roberts, and Ivo Vlaev, "Menu Positions Influence Soft Drink Selection at Touchscreen Kiosks," *Psychology & Marketing* 36, no. 10 (2019): 964–970.

19. Steven D. Levitt and John A. List, "On the Generalizability of Lab Behaviour to the Field," *Canadian Journal of Economics/Revue canadienne d'économique* 40, no. 2 (2007): 347–370.

20. Michael Hallsworth, "New Ways of Understanding Tax Compliance: From the Laboratory to the Real World," in *The Cambridge Handbook of Psychology and Economic Behaviour*, ed. Alan Lewis (Cambridge: Cambridge University Press, 2018), 430–451.

21. The Pensions Regulator, *Automatic Enrolment Commentary and Analysis: April 2018–March 2019* (Brighton, UK: The Pensions Regulator, 2019).

22. Michael Hallsworth, Tim Chadborn, Anna Sallis, Michael Sanders, Daniel Berry, Felix Greaves, Lara Clements, and Sally C. Davies, "Provision of Social Norm Feedback to High Prescribers of Antibiotics in General Practice: A Pragmatic National Randomised Controlled Trial," *Lancet* 387, no. 10029 (2016): 1743–1752; Daniella Meeker, Jeffrey A. Linder, Craig R. Fox, Mark W. Friedberg, Stephen D. Persell, Noah J. Goldstein, Tara K. Knight, Joel W. Hay, and Jason N. Doctor, "Effect of Behavioral Interventions on Inappropriate Antibiotic Prescribing among Primary Care Practices: A Randomized Clinical Trial," *JAMA* 315, no. 6 (2016): 562–570.

23. Peter Bergman and Eric W. Chan, "Leveraging Parents through Low-Cost Technology: The Impact of High-Frequency Information on Student Achievement" (New York: Columbia University Working Paper, 2019).

24. Organisation for Economic Co-operation and Development, *Behavioural Insights and Public Policy: Lessons from Around the World* (Paris: OECD Publishing, 2017).

**Chapter 2**

1. Michael Hallsworth and Elspeth Kirkman, "A Tale of Two Systems: What Can Behavioral Science Learn From Literature?," *The Behavioral Scientist* (blog), October 27, 2018.

2. John Stuart Mill, "On the Definition of Political Economy; and on the Method of Philosophical Investigation in That Science," *London and Westminster Review* 4, no. 26 (1836): 1–29.

3. The theory of utilitarianism attempted to address this issue by prioritizing "the greatest happiness of the greatest number." However, we are primarily interested in the concept of individuals maximizing their utility, as taken up by economists.

4. Joseph Persky, "The Ethology of Homo Economicus," *Journal of Economic Perspectives* 9, no. 2 (1995): 221–231.

5. Edward P. Lazear, "Economic Imperialism," *Quarterly Journal of Economics* 115, no. 1 (2000): 99–146.

6. Herbert A. Simon, *Models of Man; Social and Rational* (New York: John Wiley & Sons, 1957).

7. Richard H. Thaler, *Misbehaving: The Making of Behavioral Economics* (New York: W. W. Norton, 2015).

8. Amos Tversky and Daniel Kahneman, "Judgment under Uncertainty: Heuristics and Biases," *Science* 185, no. 4157 (1974): 1124–1131.

9. Daniel Kahneman, *Thinking, Fast and Slow* (New York: Farrar, Straus & Giroux, 2011).

10. Amos Tversky and Daniel Kahneman. "Availability: A Heuristic for Judging Frequency and Probability," *Cognitive Psychology* 5, no. 2 (1973): 207–232.

11. Barbara J. McNeil, Stephen G. Pauker, Harold C. Sox Jr., and Amos Tversky, "On the Elicitation of Preferences for Alternative Therapies," *New England Journal of Medicine* 306, no. 21 (1982): 1259.

12. Justine S. Hastings and Jesse M. Shapiro, "Fungibility and Consumer Choice: Evidence from Commodity Price Shocks," *Quarterly Journal of Economics* 128, no. 4 (2013): 1449–1498.

13. George A. Akerlof and Robert J. Shiller, "How 'Animal Spirits' Destabilize Economies," *McKinsey Quarterly* 3 (2009): 127–135.

14. Josseph Henrich, Robert Boyd, Samuel Bowles, Colin Camerer, Ernst Fehr, Herbert Gintis, and Richard McElreath, "In Search of Homo Economicus: Behavioral Experiments in 15 Small-Scale Societies," *American Economic Review* 91, no. 2 (2001): 73–78.

15. Eric J. Johnson and Daniel Goldstein, "Medicine: Do Defaults Save Lives?" *Science* 302, no. 5649 (2003): 1338–1339.

16. Richard H. Thaler and Shlomo Benartzi, "Save More Tomorrow™: Using Behavioral Economics to Increase Employee Saving," *Journal of Political Economy* 112, no. S1 (2004): S164–187.

17. William James, *The Principles of Psychology*, vol. 1 (London: Macmillan, 1890).

18. Alan G. Sanfey and Luke J. Chang, "Multiple Systems in Decision Making," *Annals of the New York Academy of Sciences* 1128, no. 1 (2008): 53–62.

19. John A. Bargh and Tanya L. Chartrand, "The Unbearable Automaticity of Being," *American Psychologist* 54, no. 7 (1999): 462–479.

20. Colin Camerer, George Loewenstein, and Drazen Prelec, "Neuroeconomics: How Neuroscience Can Inform Economics," *Journal of Economic Literature* 43, no. 1 (2005): 9–64; Matthew D. Lieberman, "Social Cognitive Neuroscience: A Review of Core Processes," *Annual Review of Psychology* 58 (2007): 259–289.

21. Thaler and Sunstein, *Nudge*.

22. Peter M. Todd and Gerd Gigerenzer, *Ecological Rationality: Intelligence in the World* (Oxford: Oxford University Press, 2012).

23. Ralph Hertwig and Till Grüne-Yanoff, "Nudging and Boosting: Steering or Empowering Good Decisions," *Perspectives on Psychological Science* 12, no. 6 (2017): 973–986.

24. Roger E. Backhouse, *The Penguin History of Economics* (London: Penguin, 2002).

25. Gary S. Becker, "Crime and Punishment: An Economic Approach," in *The Economic Dimensions of Crime, ed. Nigel G. Fielding, Alan Clarke, and Robert Witt* (London: Palgrave Macmillan, 1968), 13–68.

26. Aaron Chalfin, Benjamin Hansen, Jason Lerner, and Lucie Parker, "Reducing Crime through Environmental Design: Evidence from a Randomized Experiment of Street Lighting in New York City," NBER Working Paper 25798 (Cambridge, MA: National Bureau of Economic Research, 2019).

27. Rüdiger Graf, "Nudging Before the Nudge? Behavioural Traffic Safety Regulation and the Rise of Behavioural Economics," in *Handbook of Behavioural*

*Change and Public Policy* (Northampton, MA: Elgaronline, 2019), 23, https://doi.org/10.4337/9781785367854.

28. Jessica Pykett, Rhys Jones, and Mark Whitehead, eds., *Psychological Governance and Public Policy: Governing the Mind, Brain and Behaviour* (London: Taylor & Francis, 2016).

29. Erich Kirchler, *The Economic Psychology of Tax Behaviour* (New York: Cambridge University Press, 2007).

30. Annette Boaz and Huw Davies, eds., *What Works Now? Evidence-Informed Policy and Practice* (Bristol, UK: Policy Press, 2019).

31. Technically, nudging and libertarian paternalism are not identical (Pelle Guldborg Hansen, "The Definition of Nudge and Libertarian Paternalism: Does the Hand Fit the Glove?" *European Journal of Risk Regulation* 7, no. 1 [2016]: 155–174). However, this requires a longer discussion.

32. Cass Sunstein, *Simpler: The Future of Government* (New York: Simon & Schuster, 2013).

33. Rhys Jones, Jessica Pykett, and Mark Whitehead, *Changing Behaviours: On the Rise of the Psychological State* (Cheltenham: Edward Elgar Publishing, 2013).

34. Prime Minister's Strategy Unit, *Personal Responsibility and Changing Behaviour: The State of Knowledge and Its Implications for Public Policy* (London: HMSO, 2004).

35. David Halpern, *Inside the Nudge Unit: How Small Changes Can Make a Big Difference* (London: Random House, 2015).

36. MINDSPACE actually produces the anagram PANDEMICS, which was noted and—probably wisely—rejected.

37. Adam Oliver, *The Origins of Behavioural Public Policy* (Cambridge: Cambridge University Press, 2017), 113.

38. Holger Straßheim and Silke Beck, eds., *Handbook of Behavioural Change and Public Policy* (Cheltenham: Edward Elgar Publishing, 2019).

39. George Osborne and Richard Thaler, "We Can Make You Behave," *Guardian* 28 (2010); Richard H. Thaler, *Misbehaving: The Making of Behavioral Economics* (New York: W. W. Norton, 2015).

40. The Conservative Party, *Regulation in the Post-bureaucratic Age* (London: The Conservatives, 2009), 3.

41. The authors were early members of the BIT and still work there.

42. Peter John, *How Far to Nudge? Assessing Behavioural Public Policy* (Cheltenham: Edward Elgar Publishing, 2018).

43. Halpern, *Inside the Nudge Unit*.

44. Laura Haynes, Ben Goldacre, and David Torgerson, "Test, Learn, Adapt: Developing Public Policy with Randomised Controlled Trials" (London: Cabinet Office, 2012).

45. Sarah Ball and Joram Feitsma, "The Boundaries of Behavioural Insights: Observations from Two Ethnographic Studies," *Evidence & Policy: A Journal of Research, Debate and Practice* (2019), https://doi.org/10.1332/1744264 19X15643724702722.

46. Oliver, *Origins of Behavioural Public Policy*, 113.

47. Straßheim and Beck, *Handbook of Behavioural Change and Public Policy*.

48. Straßheim and Beck, *Handbook of Behavioural Change and Public Policy*.

49. William J. Congdon and Maya Shankar, "The White House Social & Behavioral Sciences Team: Lessons Learned From Year One," *Behavioral Science & Policy* 1, no. 2 (2015): 77–86.

50. Mark Whitehead, Rhys Jones and Jessica Pykett, "Nudging around the World: A Critical Geography of the Behaviour Change Agenda," in *Handbook of Behavioural Change and Public Policy*, 90–101.

51. Organisation for Economic Co-operation and Development, *Behavioural Insights and New Approaches to Policy Design. The Views from the Field* (Paris: OECD Publishing, 2015).

52. Organisation for Economic Co-operation and Development, *Behavioural Insights and Public Policy*.

53. Rachel Bowlby, *Shopping with Freud* (London: Routledge, 2006). Tim E. Kasser and Allen D. Kanner, *Psychology and Consumer Culture: The Struggle for a Good Life in a Materialistic World* (Washington, DC: American Psychological Association, 2004).

54. Jim Manzi, *Uncontrolled: The Surprising Payoff of Trial-and-Error for Business, Politics, and Society* (New York: Basic Books, 2012).

55. Rembrand Koning, Sharique Hasan, and Aaron Chatterji, *Experimentation and Startup Performance: Evidence from A/B Testing*, no. w26278 (Cambridge, MA: National Bureau of Economic Research, 2019).

56. Sherry Jueyu Wu and Elizabeth Levy Paluck, "Designing Nudges for the Context: Golden Coin Decals Nudge Workplace Behavior in China," *Organizational Behavior and Human Decision Processes* (2018). https://doi.org/10.1016/j.obdhp.2018.10.002.

57. Iris Bohnet, *What Works* (Cambridge, MA: Harvard University Press, 2016).

58. Greer K. Gosnell, John A. List, and Robert D Metcalfe, "The Impact of Management Practices on Employee Productivity: A Field Experiment with

Airline Captains," *Journal of Political Economy* 128, no. 4 (2020), https://doi.org/10.1086/705375.

59. Ralph Hertwig and Till Grüne-Yanoff. "Nudging and Boosting: Steering or Empowering Good Decisions," *Perspectives on Psychological Science* 12, no. 6 (2017): 973–986; Owain Service and Rory Gallagher, *Think Small: The Surprisingly Simple Ways to Reach Big Goals* (London: Michael O'Mara Books, 2017).

60. Alison W. Brooks, "Get Excited: Reappraising Pre-Performance Anxiety as Excitement," *Journal of Experimental Psychology: General* 143, no. 3 (2014): 1144.

## Chapter 3

1. Daniel Pichert and Konstantinos V. Katsikopoulos, "Green Defaults: Information Presentation and Pro-Environmental Behaviour," *Journal of Environmental Psychology* 28, no. 1 (2008): 63–73.

2. Jean Galbraith, "Treaty Options: Towards a Behavioral Understanding of Treaty Design," *Virginia Journal of International Law* 53 (2012): 309–363.

3. Brett Theodos, Christina P. Stacy, Margaret Simms, Katya Abazajian, Rebecca Daniels, Devlin Hanson, Amanda Hahnel, and Joanna Smith-Ramani, "An Evaluation of the Impacts of Two 'Rules of Thumb' for Credit Card Revolvers" (Washington, DC: Urban Institute, 2016).

4. Alejandro Drexler, Greg Fischer, and Antoinette Schoar, "Keeping It Simple: Financial Literacy and Rules of Thumb," *American Economic Journal: Applied Economics* 6, no. 2 (2014): 1–31.

5. Nava Ashraf, Oriana Bandiera, and B. Kelsey Jack, "No Margin, No Mission? A Field Experiment on Incentives for Public Service Delivery," *Journal of Public Economics* 120 (2014): 1–17.

6. Jeffrey T. Kullgren, Andrea B. Troxel, George Loewenstein, David A. Asch, Laurie A. Norton, Lisa Wesby, Yuanyuan Tao, Jingsan Zhu, and Kevin G. Volpp, "Individual- versus Group-Based Financial Incentives for Weight Loss: A Randomized, Controlled Trial," *Annals of Internal Medicine* 158, no. 7 (2013): 505–514.

7. Michael Hallsworth, John A. List, Robert D. Metcalfe, and Ivo Vlaev, "The Behavioralist as Tax Collector: Using Natural Field Experiments to Enhance Tax Compliance," *Journal of Public Economics* 148 (2017): 14–31.

8. Elizabeth Linos, "More Than Public Service: A Field Experiment on Job Advertisements and Diversity in the Police," *Journal of Public Administration Research and Theory* 28, no. 1 (2017): 67–85.

9. Adam M. Grant and David A. Hofmann, "Outsourcing Inspiration: The Performance Effects of Ideological Messages from Leaders and Beneficiaries,"

*Organizational Behavior and Human Decision Processes* 116, no. 2 (2011): 173–187.

10. Jonathan Meer, "Brother, Can You Spare a Dime? Peer Pressure in Charitable Solicitation," *Journal of Public Economics* 95, no. 7–8 (2011): 926–941; Dean Karlan and John A. List, *How Can Bill and Melinda Gates Increase Other People's Donations to Fund Public Goods?* no. w17954 (Cambridge, MA: National Bureau of Economic Research, 2012).

11. Johanna Catherine Maclean, John Buckell, and Joachim Marti, *Information Source and Cigarettes: Experimental Evidence on the Messenger Effect*, no. w25632 (Cambridge, MA: National Bureau of Economic Research, 2019).

12. Scott S. Boddery and Jeff Yates, "Do Policy Messengers Matter? Majority Opinion Writers as Policy Cues in Public Agreement with Supreme Court Decisions," *Political Research Quarterly* 67, no. 4 (2014): 851–863.

13. John Austin, Sigurdur Oli Sigurdsson, and Yonata Shpak Rubin, "An Examination of the Effects of Delayed Versus Immediate Prompts on Safety Belt Use," *Environment and Behavior* 38, no. 1 (2006): 140–149.

14. International Labor Organization, "World Statistic," 2019 (accessed January 30, 2020), https://www.ilo.org/moscow/areas-of-work/occupational -safety-and-health/WCMS_249278/lang--en/index.htm.

15. Sherry Jueyu Wu and Elizabeth Levy Paluck, "Designing Nudges for the Context: Golden Coin Decals Nudge Workplace Behavior in China," *Organizational Behavior and Human Decision Processes* (2018), https://doi.org/ 10.1016/j.obdhp.2018.10.002.

16. Donald A. Redelmeier, Joel Katz, and Daniel Kahneman, "Memories of Colonoscopy: A Randomized Trial," *Pain* 104, no. 1–2 (2003): 187–194.

## Chapter 4

1. Organisation for Economic Co-operation and Development, *Tools and Ethics for Applied Behavioural Insights: The BASIC Toolkit* (Paris: OECD, 2019).

2. Michael Sanders and Elspeth Kirkman, "I've Booked You a Place, Good Luck: A Field Experiment Applying Behavioral Science to Improve Attendance at High Impact Recruitment Events," *Journal of Behavioral Public Administration* 2, no. 1 (2019), https://doi.org/10.30636/jbpa.21.24.

3. Susan Michie, Maartje M. Van Stralen, and Robert West, "The Behaviour Change Wheel: A New Method for Characterising and Designing Behaviour Change Interventions," *Implementation Science* 6, no. 1 (2011): 42.

4. Michael Hallsworth, Mark Egan, Jill Rutter, and Julian McCrae, *Behavioural Government: Using Behavioural Science to Improve How Governments*

*Make Decisions* (London: The Behavioural Insights Team, 2018), https:///www
.bi.team.

5. Peter Leopold S. Bergman and Todd Rogers, "The Impact of Defaults on
Technology Adoption, and its Underappreciation by Policymakers," CESifo
Working Paper no. 6721, 2017.

6. Behavioral Insights Team, "EAST: Four Simple Ways to Apply Behavioural
Insights" (London: The Behavioural Insights Team, 2014).

7. Dean Karlan, Melanie Morten, and Jonathan Zinman, "A Personal Touch:
Text Messaging for Loan Repayment," National Bureau of Economic Research,
no. w17952, 2012.

8. Marco Caliendo, Deborah A. Cobb-Clark, and Arne Uhlendorff, "Locus of
Control and Job Search Strategies." *Review of Economics and Statistics* 97, no.
1 (2015): 88–103.

9. Elisabetta Sagone and Maria Elvira De Caroli, "Locus of Control and Academic Self-Efficacy in University Students: The Effects of Self-Concepts,"
*Procedia—Social and Behavioral Sciences* 114, no. 21 (2014): 222–228.

10. Michael Sanders, Guglielmo Briscese, Rory Gallagher, Alex Gyani, Samuel
Hanes, and Elspeth Kirkman, "Behavioural Insight and the Labour Market: Evidence from a Pilot Study and a Large Stepped-Wedge Controlled Trial," *Journal
of Public Policy* (2019): 1–24, https://doi.org/10.1017/S0143814X19000242.

**Chapter 5**

1. David Hagmann, Emily H. Ho, and George Loewenstein, "Nudging Out
Support for a Carbon Tax," *Nature Climate Change* 9 (2019): 484–489.

2. Matteo M. Galizzi, and Lorraine Whitmarsh, "How to Measure Behavioral
Spillovers: A Methodological Review and Checklist," *Frontiers in Psychology* 10
(2019): 342.

3. John Beshears, James J. Choi, David Laibson, Brigitte C. Madrian, and William L. Skimmyhorn, *Borrowing to Save? The Impact of Automatic Enrollment on
Debt*, no. w25876 (Cambridge, MA: National Bureau of Economic Research,
2019).

4. Dietrich Dörner, *The Logic of Failure: Recognizing and Avoiding Error in Complex Situations* (New York: Basic Books, 1996); Raymond Fisman and Miriam
A. Golden, *Corruption: What Everyone Needs to Know* (New York: Oxford University Press, 2017).

5. Dora L. Costa and Matthew E. Kahn, "Energy Conservation 'Nudges' and
Environmentalist Ideology: Evidence from a Randomized Residential Electricity Field Experiment," *Journal of the European Economic Association* 11, no. 3
(2013): 680–702.

6. Theo Lorenc, Mark Petticrew, Vivian Welch, and Peter Tugwell, "What Types of Interventions Generate Inequalities? Evidence from Systematic Reviews," *Journal of Epidemiology and Community Health* 67, no. 2 (2013): 190–193.

7. Jonathan Cribb and Carl Emmerson, "What Happens to Workplace Pension Saving When Employers Are Obliged to Enrol Employees Automatically?" *International Tax and Public Finance* (2019): 1–30.

8. Hunt Allcott and Todd Rogers, "The Short-Run and Long-Run Effects of Behavioral Interventions: Experimental Evidence from Energy Conservation," *American Economic Review* 104, no. 10 (2014): 3003–3037.

9. Michael Hallsworth, John A. List, Robert D. Metcalfe, and Ivo Vlaev, "The Behavioralist as Tax Collector: Using Natural Field Experiments to Enhance Tax Compliance," *Journal of Public Economics* 148 (2017): 14–31.

10. Alan S. Gerber, Donald P. Green, and Ron Shachar, "Voting May Be Habit-Forming: Evidence from a Randomized Field Experiment," *American Journal of Political Science* 47, no. 3 (2003): 540–550.

11. Gary Charness and Uri Gneezy, "Incentives to Exercise," *Econometrica* 77, no. 3 (2009): 909–931.

12. Katherine L. Milkman, Julia A. Minson, and Kevin G. M. Volpp, "Holding the Hunger Games Hostage at the Gym: An Evaluation of Temptation Bundling," *Management Science* 60, no. 2 (2013): 283–299.

13. Kelli A. Bird, Benjamin L. Castleman, Jeffrey T. Denning, Joshua Goodman, Cait Lamberton, and Kelly Ochs Rosinger, *Nudging at Scale: Experimental Evidence From FAFSA Completion Campaigns*, no. w26158 (Cambridge, MA: National Bureau of Economic Research, 2019).

14. Gerd Gigerenzer, "The Psychology of Good Judgment: Frequency Formats and Simple Algorithms," *Medical Decision Making* 16, no. 3 (1996): 273–280.

15. Till Grüne-Yanoff and Ralph Hertwig, "Nudge Versus Boost: How Coherent Are Policy and Theory?" *Minds and Machines* 26, no. 1–2 (2016): 149–183.

16. Will Leggett, "The Politics of Behaviour Change: Nudge, Neoliberalism and the State," *Policy & Politics* 42, no. 1 (2014): 3–19.

17. Joram Feitsma, "The Behavioural State: Critical Observations on Technocracy and Psychocracy," *Policy Sciences* 51, no. 3 (2018): 387–410.

18. Michael Muthukrishna and Joseph Henrich, "A Problem in Theory," *Nature Human Behaviour* 3 (2019): 221–229.

19. Joseph Henrich, Steven J. Heine, and Ara Norenzayan, "Beyond WEIRD: Towards a Broad-Based Behavioral Science," *Behavioral and Brain Sciences* 33, nos. 2–3 (2010): 111.

20.  Dorsa Amir, Matthew R. Jordan, Katherine McAuliffe, Claudia R. Valeggia, Lawrence S. Sugiyama, Richard G. Bribiescas, J. Josh Snodgrass, and Yarrow Dunham, "The Developmental Origins of Risk and Time Preferences Across Diverse Societies," *Journal of Experimental Psychology: General* (2019), https://doi.org/10.1037/xge0000675.

21.  Joseph Henrich, Robert Boyd, Samuel Bowles, Colin Camerer, Ernst Fehr, Herbert Gintis, Richard McElreath, et al., "'Economic Man' in Cross-Cultural Perspective: Behavioral Experiments in 15 Small-Scale Societies," *Behavioral and Brain Sciences* 28, no. 6 (2005): 795–815.

22.  Walter Mischel, Yuichi Shoda, and Philip K. Peake, "The Nature of Adolescent Competencies Predicted by Preschool Delay of Gratification," *Journal of Personality and Social Psychology* 54, no. 4 (1988): 687.

23.  Anuja Pandey, Daniel Hale, Shikta Das, Anne-Lise Goddings, Sarah-Jayne Blakemore, and Russell M. Viner, "Effectiveness of Universal Self-Regulation–Based Interventions in Children and Adolescents: A Systematic Review and Meta-Analysis," *JAMA Pediatrics* 172, no. 6 (2018): 566–575.

24.  Tyler W. Watts, Greg J. Duncan, and Haonan Quan, "Revisiting the Marshmallow Test: A Conceptual Replication Investigating Links between Early Delay of Gratification and Later Outcomes," *Psychological Science* 29, no. 7 (2018): 1159–1177.

25.  See also Armin Falk, Fabian Kosse, and Pia Pinger, "Revisiting the Marshmallow Test: On the Interpretation of Replication Results," *Psychological Science* (in press).

26.  Rachid Laajaj, Karen Macours, Daniel Alejandro Pinzon Hernandez, Omar Arias, Samuel D. Gosling, Jeff Potter, Marta Rubio-Codina, and Renos Vakis, "Challenges to Capture the Big Five Personality Traits in Non-WEIRD Populations," *Science Advances* 5, no. 7 (2019): eaaw5226.

27.  Joan E. Sieber, ed., *The Ethics of Social Research: Surveys and Experiments* (New York: Springer Science & Business Media, 2012). See also Evan Selinger, Jules Polonetsky, and Omer Tene, eds., *The Cambridge Handbook of Consumer Privacy* (New York: Cambridge University Press, 2018).

28.  Arunesh Mathur, Gunes Acar, Michael J. Friedman, Elena Lucherini, Jonathan Mayer, Marshini Chetty, and Arvind Narayanan, "Dark Patterns at Scale: Findings from a Crawl of 11K Shopping Websites," *Proceedings of the ACM on Human-Computer Interaction* 3, no. CSCW (2019): 81.

29.  Pamela Herd and Donald P. Moynihan, *Administrative Burden: Policymaking by Other Means* (New York: Russell Sage Foundation, 2019).

30.  Mark White, *The Manipulation of Choice: Ethics and Libertarian Paternalism* (New York: Palgrave, 2013).

31. Nick Chater, *The Mind Is Flat: The Illusion of Mental Depth and the Improvised Mind* (London: Penguin UK, 2018).

32. Jeremy Waldron, "It's All for Your Own Good," *New York Review of Books*, October 9, 2014, https://www.nybooks.com/articles/2014/10/09/cass-sunstein-its-all-your-own-good/.

33. Michael Sanders, Veerle Snijders, and Michael Hallsworth, "Behavioural Science and Policy: Where Are We Now and Where Are We Going?" *Behavioural Public Policy* 2, no. 2 (2018): 144–167.

34. John Stuart Mill, *On Liberty* (London: J. W. Parker & Son, 1859).

35. Thaler and Sunstein, *Nudge*.

36. Michael Hallsworth and Michael Sanders, "Nudge: Recent Developments in Behavioural Science and Public Policy," in *Beyond Behaviour Change: Key Issues, Interdisciplinary Approaches and Future Directions*, ed. Fiona Spotswood (Bristol: Policy Press, 2016), 113–133.

37. Sanders, Snijders, and Hallsworth, "Behavioural Science and Policy."

38. Luc Bovens, "The Ethics of Nudge," in *Preference Change*, ed. T. Grüne-Yanoff and Sven Ove Hansson (Dordrecht: Springer, 2009), 207–219.

39. Emily Pronin, Daniel Y. Lin, and Lee Ross, "The Bias Blind Spot: Perceptions of Bias in Self versus Others," *Personality and Social Psychology Bulletin* 28, no. 3 (2002): 369–381.

40. Emily Pronin and Kathleen Schmidt, "Claims and Denials of Bias and Their Implications for Policy," in *The Behavioral Foundations of Public Policy*, ed. E. Shafir (Princeton, NJ: Princeton University Press, 2013), 195–216.

41. Eric Luis Uhlmann and Geoffrey L. Cohen, "'I Think It, Therefore It's True': Effects of Self-Perceived Objectivity on Hiring Discrimination," *Organizational Behavior and Human Decision Processes* 104, no. 2 (2007): 207–223.

42. George Loewenstein, Cindy Bryce, David Hagmann, and Sachin Rajpal, "Warning: You Are about to Be Nudged," *Behavioral Science & Policy* 1, no. 1 (2015): 35–42.

43. Nuffield Council on Bioethics, *Public Health: Ethical Issues* (London: Nuffield Council on Bioethics, 2007).

44. Peter A. Ubel and Meredith B. Rosenthal, "Beyond Nudges—When Improving Health Calls for Greater Assertiveness," *New England Journal of Medicine* 380, no. 4 (2019): 309–311.

45. Luc Bovens terms this "token interference transparency."

46. Hansen and Jespersen have produced a useful framework that uses this insight to create four categories of nudges, depending on whether they activate the reflective system or not and whether they are transparent or not. Pelle

Guldborg Hansen and Andreas Maaløe Jespersen, "Nudge and the Manipulation of Choice: A Framework for the Responsible Use of the Nudge Approach to Behaviour Change in Public Policy," *European Journal of Risk Regulation* 4, no. 1 (2013): 3–28.

47. Keith Hawton, Helen Bergen, Sue Simkin, Sue Dodd, Phil Pocock, William Bernal, David Gunnell, and Navneet Kapur, "Long Term Effect of Reduced Pack Sizes of Paracetamol on Poisoning Deaths and Liver Transplant Activity in England and Wales: Interrupted Time Series Analyses," *BMJ* 346 (2013): 403.

48. Keith Hawton, Christopher Ware, Hamant Mistry, Jonathan Hewitt, Stephen Kingsbury, Dave Roberts, and Heather Weitzel, "Why Patients Choose Paracetamol for Self Poisoning and Their Knowledge of Its Dangers," *BMJ* 310, no. 6973 (1995): 164. In this case there was actually evidence regarding strength of intention. Interviews with people who had been admitted with paracetamol overdoses showed that the act was impulsive and based on easy availability.

49. Cass R. Sunstein, Lucia A. Reisch, and Micha Kaiser, "Trusting Nudges? Lessons from an International Survey," *Journal of European Public Policy* 26, no. 10 (2019): 1417–1443.

50. David Tannenbaum, Craig R. Fox, and Todd Rogers, "On the Misplaced Politics of Behavioural Policy Interventions," *Nature Human Behaviour* 1, no. 7 (2017): 130.

51. Joe Soss and Sanford F. Schram, "A Public Transformed? Welfare Reform as Policy Feedback," *American Political Science Review* 101, no. 1 (2007): 111–127.

52. Mark Whitehead, Rhys Jones, Rachel Lilley, Jessica Pykett, and Rachel Howell, *Neuroliberalism: Behavioural Government in the Twenty-First Century* (Abingdon: Routledge, 2017).

**Chapter 6**

1. Michael Sanders, Veerle Snijders, and Michael Hallsworth, "Behavioural Science and Policy: Where Are We Now and Where Are We Going?" *Behavioural Public Policy* 2, no. 2 (2018): 144–167.

2. Holger Straßheim and Silke Beck, eds., *Handbook of Behavioural Change and Public Policy* (Cheltenham: Edward Elgar Publishing, 2019).

3. Pelle Guldborg Hansen, "The Definition of Nudge and Libertarian Paternalism: Does the Hand Fit the Glove?" *European Journal of Risk Regulation* 7, no. 1 (2016): 155–174.

4. Caitlin Dewey, "Why the British Soda Tax Might Work Better Than Any of the Soda Taxes That Came Before It," *Washington Post*, March 21, 2018, https://www.washingtonpost.com/news/wonk/wp/2018/03/21/why-the-british-soda-tax-might-work-better-than-any-of-the-soda-taxes-that-came-before-it.

5. Denis Hummel and Alexander Maedche, "How Effective Is Nudging? A Quantitative Review on the Effect Sizes and Limits of Empirical Nudging Studies," *Journal of Behavioral and Experimental Economics* 80 (2019): 47–58.

6. Romain Cadario and Pierre Chandon, "Which Healthy Eating Nudges Work Best? A Meta-Analysis of Field Experiments," *Marketing Science* (in press).

7. Avni Shah, Matthew Osborne, Jaclyn Lefkowitz, Alissa Fishbane, and Dilip Soman, "Can Making Family Salient Increase Financial Savings? Quantifying Heterogeneous Treatment Effects in Voluntary Retirement Contributions Using a Field Experiment in Mexico" (September 25, 2019). Available at SSRN: https://ssrn.com/abstract=3460722 or http://dx.doi.org/10.2139/ssrn.3460722.

8. David Yaffe-Bellany, "Would You Like Fries with That? McDonald's Already Knows the Answer," *New York Times*, October 28, 2019, https://www.nytimes.com/2019/10/22/business/mcdonalds-tech-artificial-intelligence-machine-learning-fast-food.html.

9. Rene van Bavel and François J. Dessart, "The Case for Qualitative Methods in Behavioural Studies for EU Policy-Making," JRC Science for Policy Report, European Commission, https://ec.europa.eu/jrc/en/publication/eur-scientific-and-technical-research-reports/case-qualitative-methods-behavioural-studies-eu-policy-making (2018).

10. Rhys Jones, Jessica Pykett, and Mark Whitehead, *Changing Behaviours: On the Rise of the Psychological State* (Cheltenham: Edward Elgar Publishing, 2013).

11. Donald A. Norman, *The Psychology of Everyday Things* (New York: Basic Books, 1988).

12. Sara B. Heller, Anuj K. Shah, Jonathan Guryan, Jens Ludwig, Sendhil Mullainathan, and Harold A. Pollack, "Thinking, Fast and Slow? Some Field Experiments to Reduce Crime and Dropout in Chicago," *Quarterly Journal of Economics* 132, no. 1 (2017): 1–54.

13. Thaler and Sunstein, *Nudge*.

14. Gerd Gigerenzer, "I Think, Therefore I Err," *Social Research: An International Quarterly* 72, no. 1 (2005): 195–218.

15. Mark E. Button, "Bounded Rationality without Bounded Democracy: Nudges, Democratic Citizenship, and Pathways for Building Civic Capacity," *Perspectives on Politics* 16, no. 4 (2018): 1034–1052.

16. Cass R. Sunstein, and Reid Hastie, *Wiser: Getting Beyond Groupthink to Make Groups Smarter* (Boston: Harvard Business Press, 2015).

17. Hugo Mercier and Hélene Landemore, "Reasoning Is for Arguing: Understanding the Successes and Failures of Deliberation," *Political Psychology* 33, no. 2 (2012): 243–258.

18. Christian R. Grose, "Field Experimental Work on Political Institutions," *Annual Review of Political Science* 17 (2014): 355–370; Brendan Nyhan and Jason Reifler, "The Effect of Fact-Checking on Elites: A Field Experiment on US State Legislators," *American Journal of Political Science* 59, no. 3 (2015): 628–640.

19. Michael Hallsworth, "How Complexity Economics Can Improve Government: Rethinking Policy Actors, Institutions and Structures," in *Complex New World: Translating New Economic Thinking into Public Policy* (London: IPPR [Institute for Public Policy Research], 2012), 39–49.

20. Michael Macy, Sebastian Deri, Alexander Ruch, and Natalie Tong, "Opinion Cascades and the Unpredictability of Partisan Polarization," *Science Advances* 5, no. 8 (2019): eaax0754.

21. Matthew J. Salganik, Peter Sheridan Dodds, and Duncan J. Watts, "Experimental Study of Inequality and Unpredictability in an Artificial Cultural Market," *Science* 311, no. 5762 (2006): 854–856.

22. Gerlinde Fellner, Rupert Sausgruber, and Christian Traxler, "Testing Enforcement Strategies in the Field: Threat, Moral Appeal and Social Information," *Journal of the European Economic Association* 11, no. 3 (2013): 634–660.

23. Francesco Drago, Friederike Mengel, and Christian Traxler, "Compliance Behavior in Networks: Evidence from a Field Experiment," *American Economic Journal: Applied Economics* (in press).

24. Paul Ormerod, "Nudge Plus Networks," *RSA Journal* 156, no. 5543 (2010): 10–15.

25. Elisabeth Costa and David Halpern, "The Behavioural Science of Online Harm and Manipulation, and What to Do about It" (London: The Behavioural Insights Team, 2019), https:///www.bi.team.

26. Paul K. Presson and Victor A. Benassi, "Illusion of Control: A Meta-Analytic Review," *Journal of Social Behavior and Personality* 11, no. 3 (1996): 493.

27. Mark S. Horswill and Frank P. McKenna, "Drivers' Hazard Perception Ability: Situation Awareness on the Road," in *A Cognitive Approach to Situation*

*Awareness: Theory and Application*, ed. Simon Banbury and Sebastien Tremblay (Farnham: Ashgate, 2004), 155–175.

28. Joram Feitsma, "Brokering Behaviour Change: The Work of Behavioural Insights Experts in Government," *Policy & Politics* 47, no. 1 (2019): 37–56.

29. Michael Hallsworth, Mark Egan, Jill Rutter, and Julian McCrae, *Behavioural Government*, https:///www.bi.team.

# FURTHER READING

Akerlof, George A., and Robert J. Shiller. *Animal Spirits: How Human Psychology Drives the Economy, and Why It Matters for Global Capitalism.* Princeton, NJ: Princeton University Press, 2010.

Dolan, Paul, Michael Hallsworth, David Halpern, Dominic King, and Ivo Vlaev. *MINDSPACE: Influencing Behaviour for Public Policy.* London: Institute for Government and Cabinet Office, 2010.

Dörner, Dietrich. *The Logic of Failure: Recognizing and Avoiding Error in Complex Situations.* New York: Basic Books, 1996.

Elster, Jon. *Explaining Social Behavior: More Nuts and Bolts for the Social Sciences.* New York: Cambridge University Press, 2015.

Hallsworth, Michael, Mark Egan, Jill Rutter, and Julian McCrae. "Behavioural Government: Using Behavioural Science to Improve How Governments Make Decisions." London: The Behavioural Insights Team, 2018.

Halpern, D. *Inside the Nudge Unit: How Small Changes Can Make a Big Difference.* London: Random House, 2015.

John, Peter. *How Far to Nudge? Assessing Behavioural Public Policy.* Cheltenham: Edward Elgar Publishing, 2018.

Kahneman, Daniel. *Thinking, Fast and Slow.* New York: Farrar, Straus and Giroux, 2011.

Organisation for Economic Co-operation and Development. *Tools and Ethics for Applied Behavioural Insights: The BASIC Toolkit.* Paris: OECD, 2019.

Sugden, Robert. *The Community of Advantage: A Behavioural Economist's Defence of the Market.* Oxford: Oxford University Press, 2018.

Sunstein, Cass R., and Reid Hastie. *Wiser: Getting Beyond Groupthink to Make Groups Smarter.* Cambridge, MA: Harvard Business Press, 2015.

Thaler, Richard. *Misbehaving: The Making of Behavioral Economics.* New York: W. W. Norton, 2015.

Thaler, Richard H., and Cass R. Sunstein. *Nudge: Improving Decisions about Health, Wealth, and Happiness.* New Haven, CT: Yale University Press, 2008.

Todd, Peter M., and Gerd Gigerenzer. *Ecological Rationality: Intelligence in the World.* Oxford: Oxford University Press, 2012.

Whitehead, Mark, Rhys Jones, Rachel Lilley, Jessica Pykett, and Rachel Howell. *Neuroliberalism: Behavioural Government in the Twenty-First Century.* London: Routledge, 2017.

# INDEX

Sunstein, Cass R., 46, 48–50, 162–163. *See also Nudge*
Behavioural Insights Team (BIT) and, 56
on libertarian paternalism, 48
on nudge/nudging, 47–49, 170, 183
policy, regulation, and, 50
Superiority bias, 191

Taxation, 14, 44, 58, 76, 125, 164. *See also* Sugared drink tax
Tax compliance, 19, 44, 58, 76, 185
Temptation bundling, 130–131
Test, Learn, Adapt process, 59
Text messaging. *See* SMS
Thaler, Richard H., 31–32, 46, 48–50. *See also Nudge*
Behavioural Insights Team (BIT) and, 56
Conservative Party (UK) advised by, 55
on libertarian paternalism, 48
on mental accounting, 32
on nudge/nudging, 47–49, 57, 170, 183
Token interference transparency, 214n45
Transparency, 156, 159, 160f
token interference, 214n45
Treatment groups, 113–114
Tversky, Amos, 28–31, 36–37

Unemployment, goal of reducing, 81–83, 86, 87f
Unemployment centers, 86, 88, 92–94, 109–110, 119–122. *See also* Bedford Jobcentre

Behavioural Insights Team (BIT) and, 109–110, 121
Unemployment policy, 90
"Upstreaming" (strategic) decision making, 192–193
Utilitarianism, 26, 205n3
Utility, 30
maximizing, 26, 205n3

Validity, 140. *See also* Generalizability
Vlaev, Ivo, 51–54
Voting behavior, 130

WEIRD (Western, Educated, Industrialized, Rich, and Democratic), 140
WEIRD science and the problem of generalizability, 140–143
Workplace safety, improving by redesigning the floor space around workstations, 77–78
Wu, Sherry Jueyu, 78
Wundt, Wilhelm, 36, 39

**The MIT Press Essential Knowledge Series**

*AI Ethics*, Mark Coeckelbergh
*Algorithms*, Panos Louridas
*Annotation*, Remi H. Kalir and Antero Garcia
*Anticorruption*, Robert I. Rotberg
*Auctions*, Timothy P. Hubbard and Harry J. Paarsch
*The Book*, Amaranth Borsuk
*Behavioral Insights*, Michael Hallsworth and Elspeth Kirkman
*Carbon Capture*, Howard J. Herzog
*Citizenship*, Dimitry Kochenov
*Cloud Computing*, Nayan B. Ruparelia
*Collaborative Society*, Dariusz Jemielniak and Aleksandra Przegalinska
*Computational Thinking*, Peter J. Denning and Matti Tedre
*Computing: A Concise History*, Paul E. Ceruzzi
*The Conscious Mind*, Zoltan E. Torey
*Contraception: A Concise History*, Donna J. Drucker
*Critical Thinking*, Jonathan Haber
*Crowdsourcing*, Daren C. Brabham
*Cynicism*, Ansgar Allen
*Data Science*, John D. Kelleher and Brendan Tierney
*Deep Learning*, John D. Kelleher
*Extraterrestrials*, Wade Roush
*Extremism*, J. M. Berger
*Fake Photos,* Hany Farid
*fMRI*, Peter A. Bandettini
*Food*, Fabio Parasecoli
*Free Will*, Mark Balaguer
*The Future*, Nick Montfort
*GPS*, Paul E. Ceruzzi
*Haptics*, Lynette A. Jones
*Information and Society*, Michael Buckland
*Information and the Modern Corporation*, James W. Cortada
*Intellectual Property Strategy*, John Palfrey
*The Internet of Things*, Samuel Greengard
*Irony and Sarcasm*, Roger Kreuz
*Machine Learning: The New AI*, Ethem Alpaydin
*Machine Translation*, Thierry Poibeau
*Macroeconomics*, Felipe Larrain B.

MICHAEL HALLSWORTH, PhD, is Managing Director of the Behavioural Insights Team (BIT) North America. He is an Assistant Professor (Adjunct) at Columbia University and an Honorary Lecturer at Imperial College London.

ELSPETH KIRKMAN founded BIT's North American office before returning to the UK to run the organization's social policy portfolio out of London. She has taught behavioral insights courses at Harvard and Warwick Universities and is a Visiting Senior Research Fellow at King's College London.